Picking Up The Pieces:

A Practical Guide for Rebuilding Churches Broken By Clergy Misconduct

---

Dr. Vernon D. Shelton, Sr.

FOREWORD BY BISHOP WALTER SCOTT THOMAS, SR.

Picking Up The Pieces

Dr. Vernon D. Shelton, Sr.

Picking Up The Pieces: A Practical Guide for Rebuilding Churches Broken By Clergy Misconduct

Copyright © 2012 by Desakajo Publishing

Picking Up The Pieces

4

DEDICATION

In loving memory of my grandmother, Clara Braxton-Moore.
For my family who has supported me through this and every
major endeavor of my life.
And every church that has experienced, hurt and clergy
misconduct of any kind.

ACKNOWLEDGEMENTS

First and foremost I would like to thank my Lord and Savior Jesus Christ who has called me out of darkness into His marvelous light to serve Him as a voice in the wilderness.

I would like to thank my lovely wife, LaPrena Shelton, for her patience and support throughout my masters and doctoral journey. I could not have accomplished these great tasks without her by my side.

I am grateful to my children, Vernon Jr., Terrance, Ayona, Monique, and Myriah, for their patience and the sacrifices made while I was away at school and traveling throughout the country.

I am forever grateful for my parents, Marolyn Tucker, Vernon G. Shelton, and Lynne Saunders who always taught me that all things are possible. Thanks for loving me unconditionally.

I thank God for all of my siblings (Laticia, Scooby, Darrin, Angie, Isha, Shaquan, Sid, Kurt) for all their prayers and support.

To my cousin Troy Blackwell who started this journey with me.

I thank God for my Pastor and father in ministry, Dr. Anthony M. Chandler, Sr. for pushing me to pursue academic excellence. Thank you for being the visible model of excellence and integrity in ministry. "I am who I am, because of you."

I thank God for my first church the New Hope Christian Baptist Church in Baltimore, MD. It was a privilege to serve as pastor for five years.

Further thanks to my church family, The Holy Trinity Baptist Church, Amityville, NY. Thanks for your loving support throughout this process. It is a privilege and an honor to pastor such a wonderful people.

I thank God for all my sons and daughters in ministry. Thank you for the impact you have made on my life and pastoral journey.

I thank God for my editorial staff, Dr. Patricia McCarthy, Angela Mack-Brown and J.W. Stevenson. I thank God for the advice and wisdom of Dr. Patricia Rickenbacker and Dr. Sedgwick Easley who guided me through this process.

I thank God for my spiritual brothers in ministry who pushed me while at UTS. Dr. Steven J. Daniels, Dr. Rodney Coleman and Dr. Leandre Marshall.

I am deeply grateful for the guidance and wisdom of my UTS mentors, Dr. Daryl Hairston and Dr. Lucius Dalton. This project would not have been completed without their input and direction.

I thank God for those individuals who have been role models and mentors to me throughout my pastoral ministry. Dr. Jimmy C. Baldwin, Bishop Walter Scott Thomas, Sr., Bishop Dewayne C. Debnam, Pastor Gary G. Johnson, Dr. Elmore E. Warren, Dr. Reginald Thomas, and Bishop Oscar E. Brown.

I thank God for my friends in ministry who have been great supporters and prayer partners. Dr. Alonzo R. Smith, Brother Keith Miller, Brother Ronald McNair, Pastor Kenyan Southers, Pastor Corey Hatchett, Pastor Kevin Northam, Pastor Stephen Lawrence, and all of my Baltimore, New York, and Eastern Baptist Association brothers and sisters in ministry. Thank you for all that you have deposited in my life and ministry!

Dr. Vernon D. Shelton, Sr.

TABLE OF CONTENTS

FOREWORD

Young preachers are often criticized as being faddish, arrogant, impulsive and self-centered. Dr. Vernon D. Shelton, Sr. reminds us that we cannot stereotype a group or put everyone in the same category. Here is a young man who takes seriously the call upon his life, and challenges all of us to do the same.

Many churches have been hurt by the inappropriate actions of the pastors and leaders. No leader willing guides his or her people over a cliff. Yet, none of us can fully control the consequences of our actions, and as much, many churches are forced to live with "in intended consequences." The hurt which is done is real and leaves scars that can take years to heal. Some churches never fully recovery from their wounds. *Picking Up The Pieces* reminds us just how deep those wounds can be.

The church is the haven and headquarters of grace and while it is essential that a fallen pastor be shown grace, it is equally important that the church be nurtured back to wholeness and recovery. Pain puts a pall on ministry, while shame and hurt can cripple the fulfillment of ministry vision. When hurt has taken place, there needs to be a restorative process for the people of God. We have seen great churches fade to black because they could not recovery from a major break in ministry ethics. Dr. Shelton realizes that recovery is not just a step, it is a process. We don't just say I'm healed; we have to grow and be nurtured into our wholeness after we have been hurt.

This is a bold new process for the church. It requires the church to admit it's level of pain, and seeks the necessary steps toward healing. This work by Dr. Shelton is a guide that will enable the church to begin that process of healing and restoration. Moreover it defines defending the emotional and spiritual health of the church as critical and important. We all are wounded healers, but there must be an attempt to bandage the wounds before we bleed to death. I encourage every pastor, church leader, and hurting congregation to read this work with a renewed passion for the work of the church and its role in God's plan. Implement the checks and balances before a problem arises and trust that the plan will work. Dr. Shelton has much to say; and in this seminal work he lets us know we want to hear what he has to say.

Bishop Walter S. Thomas Sr.

Senior Pastor, New Psalmist Baptist Church, Baltimore, Md.

Presiding Prelate, Kingdom Association of Covenant Pastors

INTRODUCTION

Accepting the call as the new pastor of a congregation can be one of the most exciting moments in the life of a minister. It comes with great anticipation and expectations. However, accepting the call to pastor a church can also come with many challenges. A new pastor has to take time to learn the culture and history of the church. He or she has to get to know the different personalities and proclivities of members and leaders within the congregation. A new pastor has to uncover and prayerfully deal with the issues within the church, which the search committee fails to disclose during the interviewing process. In addition to all of this, a new pastor must gain the trust and confidence of the congregation so he or she can successfully cast vision and move the people forward. This can be a very challenging task for any new pastor. It becomes an even greater challenge for the pastor who has accepted the call to a hurting congregation, or a congregation which has experienced some form of clergy misconduct.

When a church has experienced this type of hurt, it creates additional challenges for the pastor who follows. Many times the pain of the past is taken out on the new pastor. For example, the new pastor may face doubt, distrust, resistance, skepticism and suspicion, rather than love, respect and confidence. All of which can be hard to deal with as a new pastor who has not mistreated or harmed anyone in that particular congregation.

Moreover, when a church has been hurt by some form of clergy misconduct it affects them physically, mentally and spiritually. In some instances, members lose trust not only in their former pastor, but also they feel they cannot trust another pastor. Some members leave the church altogether while others stay and attempt to hold the church together until a new pastor arrives. The overall stress and pressure of leading a hurting congregation can take a negative toll on the new pastor. It can cause the new pastor to become discouraged and disheartened toward the ministry. It can cause frustration and problems within the pastor's family. Ultimately, it can lead to his or her early resignation, prolonging healing for the congregation. With this in mind, it becomes obvious that special care and practical advice is needed for rebuilding hurting and broken congregations, especially those which have been hurt by clergy misconduct.

For these reasons, I believe this book will be a useful and effective tool for hurting churches and pastors who follow a minister whom committed some form of clergy misconduct. Ultimately, this book will give a biblical, theological and practical approach for rebuilding, healing and moving the church forward. It also gives practical advice for the new pastor to have a successful and healthy pastorate while rebuilding a hurting congregation.

The hypothesis of this book proposes that when a pastoral successor does the basic pastoral duties well, lives with integrity, develops appropriate relationships with congregants, and teaches

16

sound biblical principles, it will begin the process of restoring trust in the office of minister, restoring hope and fostering healing to a hurting congregation.

THE WOUNDED HEALER

As a child, I grew up in an urban Baltimore City neighborhood known as the Park Heights community. Park Heights was a high drug-populated area with the majority of the families living below or just above federal poverty guidelines. In spite of the numerous challenges and obstacles encountered growing up in this neighborhood, many positive relationships were formed. Although I lived in a single-parent home, with limited resources and financial limitations, I never lacked love and support. I am the youngest of three children to my mother; all of whom are two years apart. I also have three sisters and two brothers from my father. At an early age, my mother instilled in me the importance of spending time with family. She always said, "Nothing is worth more than spending time with the people you love."

Despite growing up in an area whose reputation of criminal activity preceded it, I encountered some people who influenced my life in a very positive way, such as Mr. and Mrs. Powell. The Powells epitomized the "perfect family." They spent quality time together, had dinner together every night and prayed regularly. As a child, I spent countless hours in the Powell's home. As a family, they were very active in the church. In fact, they were largely instrumental in providing the start to my Christian journey. At least five days out of the week they were in church, which in turn resulted in church becoming a regular part of my life.

As I got older, my life appeared to be going as God had planned until the persons who had been instrumental in my spiritual maturity the Powells, relocated. This was the beginning of a rough transition in my life. With the Powell's gone, no one was there pushing me to stay active in church. From that point on, my direction in life changed drastically. My teenage years were somewhat tumultuous times, as I found myself spending less time in the church and more time in the streets, doing the very things I had previously avoided.

Yet in the midst of my rebellious stage, I found a new constant in baseball. Although I had always had a passion for the sport as a child, I did not participate in organized baseball until right before high school. From that point on, I played in summer leagues on a regular basis. In many ways, baseball was everything to me. It was an outlet from my crime-infested neighborhood, which allowed me to work through my frustrations and disappointments. More importantly, playing an organized sport provided me the structure, which I needed in life. I was blessed with the opportunity to play division I baseball in college under former Oriole and Yankee center fielder Paul Blair. I was also fortunate to play in the semi-pros in Maryland.

After a sudden career-ending injury to the pitching shoulder, I permanently hung up my glove and put aside any dreams of playing in the big league. Forced to make a career shift, I went in search of traditional employment and eventually obtained a position with People Encouraging People, an organization known for providing a variety of social, mental, and educational services to low-income individuals. I did not know it then, but this move proved to be a pivotal moment in my life. For the first time, I found myself surrounded by an office full of educated Christian women. Through their example, I was inspired to revisit the Christian roots of my youth. My co-workers helped me rekindle my relationship with the Lord, urging me to attend worship services, bible studies, and other church-oriented events with them. It was not too long before the desire to have a church home overwhelmed me. I spent weeks visiting different churches throughout the city seeking one that I could call home, but this proved to be a more daunting task than I expected. Perhaps the biggest challenge I had was locating one that did not make me feel like an outsider.

During the time that I was searching for a church home, I did not own the standard "church clothes," nor was I familiar with the new way churches appeared to operate. Although many of the churches I visited were nice, I had no desire to join any of them because I did not feel welcomed. It was not until I went to visit my cousin's church to participate in my goddaughter's dedication, that I truly felt at home. When I looked around Jerusalem Baptist Church, I was impressed to see young people my age participating in the worship service. Also, the assistant pastor (Rev. Richard

Holland) took the time to engage me personally once service was over. After visiting for a few weeks, I decided to become a committed member. Shortly after completing the new member orientation process, I became involved in various ministries throughout the church. Those ministries included the youth choir, the youth and young adult ministry, the male usher board, and the Sunday school department. I also became the person God used to witness to my family. My faith in God and involvement in the church led them to join Jerusalem Baptist Church.

It was at Jerusalem Baptist Church where I received and accepted my call to preach the gospel. On March 2, 2002, I preached my initial sermon and was licensed as a minister of the Gospel. After accepting the call to ministry, my life changed immensely. I assumed the role of the spiritual leader within my family. As a result of the changes displayed in my life, many of my childhood and college friends began to seek me for spiritual guidance. While it was indeed a tremendous honor, it also added pressure for me to be an example for others to follow.

Shortly after entering the gospel ministry, I was elevated to the position of Youth and Young Adult Minister. This was an exciting and challenging assignment. I was required to lead the very individuals with whom I had previously socialized. Gradually, the Youth and Young Adult ministry started to experience growth in numerous ways. Attendance in Sunday school and bible study increased, the youth choir expanded, and a youth usher board was established. In addition, the Youth and Young Adult ministry formed an after-school mentoring program for Jerusalem's youth and the surrounding community. Subsequently, the Youth and Young Adult ministry became the catalyst largely responsible for the church's resurgence.

As the youth increased their participation in ministry, they were inspired to bring their relatives to church, which in turn, generated growth in Jerusalem's overall membership. Given the fact that the Youth and Young Adult ministry was growing and touching the lives of many, one would think that everyone, especially the pastor, would be pleased. Yet, ironically, such was not the case. This evidence of church growth seemed to be the catalyst for tension and animosity directed at me by my pastor and others at the church. Although ministry had become extremely troubling for me at Jerusalem, God had begun to open doors for me at other churches. Within the first two months of being licensed I received numerous invitations to preach at various churches throughout the city.

As time passed, the situation grew worse. Although I had only been preaching for a few months, I already felt like quitting. I heard many stories of individuals who had been hurt by their pastor or church leadership, but now I had experienced it first-hand. Hurting and lacking the support I needed at Jerusalem, I reached out to another local pastor for guidance and instruction. For the next few months, I spent time with Dr. Anthony M. Chandler Sr. who ministered to me throughout this painful process.

He encouraged me to stay faithful, and pray for my pastor, but never say anything bad about her.

After several months of praying and seeking guidance, I believed God was leading me to transition to another ministry. When I shared how I felt with my family and friends, none of them thought it was a good idea. However, I expected that type of reaction since I had never disclosed how stressful ministry had become for me at Jerusalem. When I decided that I was going to leave many members told me that if I left Jerusalem I would not make it in ministry, and that I would never be successful because "nobody wants an unstable minister." Hearing words like these from people I initially admired stung worse than a slap in the face. Yet and still I had a sense of peace with my decision, secure in the fact that I had done nothing wrong and had faithfully served. During my final meeting with my pastor I thanked her for giving me my start in ministry and wished her well as she continued to lead God's people. Even though it was one of the most painful trials I had ever experienced, it helped make my transition easier.

In August of 2002, I left Jerusalem Baptist Church and joined the New Bethlehem Baptist Church in Baltimore, Maryland under the leadership of Dr. Anthony M. Chandler, Sr. Through prayer and the support of Dr. Chandler I was able to endure one of the most emotionally draining periods of my life. While serving at New Bethlehem, I was very skeptical about building a close relationship with my new pastor. I did not want to repeat the experience I had at Jerusalem. Dr. Chandler did not deserve the skepticism. But, because of my past pain, I built a wall of protection around me. Over time, I truly got to know Dr. Chandler and saw his integrity. I removed the wall of protection and opened myself up to receive what he had to offer. This was the beginning of a healthy spiritual father and son relationship. This relationship has forever changed my life. It was through this relationship that I discovered that not all pastors are the same, and what one has done should not affect how you deal with another.

After serving at New Bethlehem Baptist Church for a number of years, I was asked to serve as the interim pastor for the New Hope Christian Baptist Church located in Baltimore City. After serving six months as the interim pastor, on March 31, 2006, I was unanimously elected as the senior pastor. This was a unique situation in that New Hope was a church which had recently experienced tremendous hurt and devastation. When I arrived at New Hope, the membership of approximately fifteen to twenty people was fighting to hold on. The church had split as a result of what they described as clergy misconduct. A sharp decline in finances produced new debts. Clearly, rebuilding such a church would be a daunting task for any pastor. The pain and hurt, which was lingering from what they had previously experienced, caused the congregation to be suspicious of the young pastor newly come to shepherd them.

Despite the mistrust and challenges I was facing, I spent my first two years preaching hope and restoration. I spent months teaching the congregation how to forgive and move beyond their pain. Because many in the congregation were sensitive and skeptical about clergy, especially young pastors, I spent a lot of time getting to know the congregation personally. I developed a ministry at-large which embraced the vision of family, healing and unity. I spent a lot of time modeling and teaching about proper relationships and boundaries. After a few years of demonstrating integrity and faithfulness in ministry, the church began to transition. The membership grew, hope was regained and financial stability was restored. In addition, it appeared that trust and respect for clergy, which had been lost, was now restored. What began as a hurting and broken church had once again became a place of love, hope and joy.

After almost five years of service at New Hope, the Lord had another assignment for me. On April 12, 2010, I was called as the new pastor of the Holy Trinity Baptist Church in Amityville, NY. After a short time at Holy Trinity, I discovered history had repeated itself. Once again I had to rebuild and restore hope to a hurting congregation.

Throughout the last twenty-three years, Holy Trinity has experienced a level of hurt, devastation and spiritual warfare which no church should have to endure. These challenges have in many ways created division and discouragement within the congregation. However, despite numerous trials and unexpected setbacks, the people of Holy Trinity have always persevered.

The Synergy

As I reflect on my life and all my ministry experiences, the need for healing and restoration emerges. As a child, when I lost someone close to me, healing was what I needed to move on. As a young minister at Jerusalem, when the relationship with my pastor fell apart, it required healing and encouragement in order to move forward. The need for healing surfaced once again with my first pastorate at the New Hope Christian Baptist Church. However, this time I was the one fostering the healing. The Lord used me to rebuild, restore hope and healing to that congregation. After five years at New Hope, God transitioned me to The Holy Trinity Baptist Church and the need for rebuilding and healing has emerged again. The issues at this church may be different from my first church, but the need for healing and rebuilding is still the same.

The connection within my life and ministry occurs at the place of hurt, healing and rebuilding. Although unbeknown to me, everything happens for a reason. Perhaps the Lord allowed me to experience painful times throughout my life and ministry so I could fully understand and empathize with others who are hurting. For it is always easier for one to believe it is possible to overcome feelings of hurt and devastation when he or she knows you have experienced it first-hand. It appears God is using me to be what renowned priest and author Henri J.M. Nouwen calls, "The Wounded Healer." It has truly become my desire to be a vessel which brings healing and restoration to churches and victims which experienced hurt due to some form of clergy misconduct.

CHAPTER ONE

THE NATURE OF CLERGY MISCONDUCT

Through the ages, churches have experienced devastating and demoralizing situations. Events such as natural disasters, hate crimes, bombings, fires, and financial hardships have all struck churches leaving them inundated with a host of problems. Another phenomenon which has traumatized the church even more than those previously mentioned is clergy misconduct. Numerous congregations suffer hurt and shame when cases of clergy misconduct surface in their church. This happens as a result of the high moral and ethical expectation of religious leaders in regards to their personal lifestyles. When clergy violate their ministerial expectations, it harms not only the victims, but the church as a whole. As a result of moral failures of clergy, churches have been sued for enormous amounts of money, publicly criticized by the media, and abandoned by victims who lost their trust in this sacred institution.

Clergy misconduct has affected the church spiritually, emotionally, and financially. Another term for clergy misconduct is clergy malfeasance.[1] Anson Shupe defines it as "the exploitation and abuse of a religious group's believers by trusted elites and leaders of that religion."[2] The three forms, or types, of clergy malfeasance or deviance, categorized by Shupe are sexual, economic and authoritative. Shupe breaks down the three categories in this manner:

> The sexual deviance category includes rape, seduction, pedophilia and ephebophilia (erotic attraction to prepubescent and adolescent children), and homosexuality. The economic deviance category includes money-making schemes, dishonest elite employees of religious organizations and con-artist television evangelists who raise money over the airwaves for missions and other purposes that do not exist. The third and most sensitive category of deviance is authoritative. This includes excessive monitoring and controlling of members' livelihoods, resources, and lifestyles for one's own personal benefit, in either money or power."[3]

Whether sexual, economic, or authoritative, clergy misconduct/clergy malfeasance occurs whenever a clergy person or religious leader violates the fiduciary relationship with his or her followers. Shupe refers to those individuals as "Bad Pastors." Bad pastors as defined by Shupe are clergy who misuse trusting people; exploit them sexually and financially; and/or manipulate them with

---

[1] Anson D. Shupe, *Wolves within the Fold: Religious Leadership and Abuses of Power* (New Brunswick, NJ: Rutgers University Press, 1998), 1.
[2] Ibid.
[3] Ibid., 6-7.

excessive demands grounded in spiritual authority.[4] Regardless of the label given to clergy misconduct, the bottom line remains that churches and those within are being hurt by individuals who fail to maintain the integrity of the position they have been entrusted to uphold.

For years, clergy misconduct, (money, power, and sex) has dominated the history of the Roman Catholic Church. It has subjugated its canon laws and been the driving force for many reforms. Now, in the 21st century, money, power and sexual misconduct in the church are still the main areas of concern. Recent polls revealed 12.67 percent of clergy who took a survey reported they had sexual intercourse with a church member. This percentage is the same across lines of denomination, theological orientation, and gender.[5] These are just a few examples of clergy misconduct in the 21st century. It is clear that clergy misconduct/clergy malfeasance is not simply an issue of the past, but rather a challenge for many congregations in the future.

The book, *In The Name of All That's Holy, A Theory of Clergy Malfeasance*, Shupe provides an overview of clergy malfeasance, as well as insight to what he believes is the cause of the problem. According to Shupe, "the problem of clergy malfeasance/clergy

---

[4] Anson D. Shupe, William A. Stacey, and Susan E. Darnell, *Bad Pastors: Clergy Misconduct in Modern America* (New York: New York University Press, 2000), 1.
[5] Marie Fortune and James N. Poling, *Sexual Abuse By Clergy, A Crisis For The Church* (Decatur, GA: Journal of Pastoral Care Publications, 1994), 5.

misconduct is as old as the practice of religion itself."[6] He reports while it has been a problem for centuries, it did not garner public attention until the last several decades. Clergy misconduct has been an issue since biblical times, but the media was not as efficient as it is today. Years ago when something happened only those who were local would be informed. Now that we have CNN, Media TakeOut, internet, Facebook, Twitter and other social networking sites, news whether true or false travels fast. Therefore, clergy misconduct is not a new issue it just started receiving more public attention.

Another useful aspect to this research was learning that clergy misconduct was not limited to a particular denomination or region of the world. Clergy misconduct is a worldwide problem. Rebekah Miles supports this point in her book, *The Pastor As Moral Guide*. In her book, she states, "No denomination or theological perspectives are immune to misconduct or the failure of accountability. The issue crosses all lines of age, wealth, ethnicity, and even gender. Though the great majority of abusers are men and most victims are women, that is not always so. Men, particularly younger men and boys, are sometimes victims, and women are sometimes perpetrators. Male and female clergy bear equal

---

[6]Anson D. Shupe, *In the Name of All That's Holy: A Theory of Clergy Malfeasance* (Westport, CT: Praeger, 1995), 41.

responsibility for holding themselves and other pastors accountable."[7]

Candace Benyei also shares this opinion via her book, *Understanding Clergy Misconduct in Religious Systems: Scapegoating Family Secrets and The Abuse of Power*. Benyei states, "The sexual misconduct of spiritual leaders is not confined to any one denomination or religious faith. North American Christians, Jews, Buddhists, Sufis, and Hindus have all experienced boundary violations of this sort in their families of faith. Partially, this is the result of personal psychology combined with authoritarian forms of social structuring. It is the result of stirring up the right side of the brain, which is cohabited by both the activities of sex and prayer-an ancient awareness and ancient struggle of all who have pursued celibate mystical paths. Sexual misconduct is a rupture of the covenant of trust between clergyperson and congregant."[8] Although these authors come from diverse backgrounds and write from different perspectives, they all agree that clergy misconduct is not limited to a particular race, denomination, ethnicity or region. This is an issue which has affected victims and churches in every faith community.

Moreover, when dealing with the topic of clergy misconduct, the bulk of the work is centered on clergy sexual abuse/sexual

---

[7] Rebekah Miles, *The Pastor as Moral Guide*, Creative Pastoral Care and Counseling (Minneapolis, MN: Fortress Press, 1999), 104.
[8] Candace Reed Benyei, *Understanding Clergy Misconduct in Religious Systems: Scapegoating, Family Secrets, and the Abuse of Power* (New York: Haworth Pastoral Press, 1998), 59.

harassment. While clergy misconduct is not limited to sexual abuse or sexual harassment, the majority of the accusations against clergy are related to these two areas. Therefore, it was imperative to study these topics in detail to obtain a clear understanding of the issues at hand. Nancy Myer Hopkins authored the book, *The Congregational Response to Clergy Betrayals of Trust,* which was particularly helpful in describing sexual harassment in detail. This data was essential to the research because an individual may be committing sexual harassment yet is unaware his or her behavior is viewed as such. According to Hopkins:

> Sexual harassment is primarily understood to occur between a church leader and a person in his or her employ, a colleague, or one being mentored by them. Included in harassment are sexualized conversations and innuendo, establishment of a hostile climate for women, unwelcome touching and hugging, pressure for dates, excluding women from meetings, sabotaging women's work, sexist jokes, hostile put-downs, public humiliation, exaggerated or mocking "courtesy," obscene or harassing phone calls, discussion of one's partner's sexual inadequacies, "accidentally" brushing sexual parts of the body, pressing or rubbing up against the victim, "full body hugs," erotic kissing, leaning over or otherwise invading another's space, sexual "sneak attacks," soliciting sexual services, stalking, and sexual assault.[9]

Another critical area which Hopkins highlights is the difference between sexual harassment and sexual exploitation. While the two

---

[9] Nancy Myer Hopkins and Interfaith Sexual Trauma Institute (Collegeville, MN), *The Congregational Response to Clergy Betrayals of Trust* (Collegeville, MN: Liturgical Press, 1998), 11.

subjects are similar, there is a difference. Harassment is understood as constituting unwanted sexual advances, whereas sexual exploitation involves a vulnerable congregant who initially might have felt confused or ambivalent about the advances.[10] Due to the amount of power the position of clergy exudes, the responsibility for maintaining the boundaries always rest with them. This is important to note because many clergy engage in relationships with congregants, but it is their job to maintain the boundaries of the ministerial relationship.

One of the challenges which some clergy struggle with is how to express their sexuality in a healthy manner yet maintain boundaries. In the book, *Sex In The Parish*, Karen Lebacqz states, "Many pastors, both male and female struggle with their sexuality and with their theology of sexuality."[11] For instance, single pastors who are dating or engaging in a sexual relationship with single congregants in their congregation. This has been an issue for many ministers based on their theology of sexuality. Some ministers feel pastors should not engage in sexual relationships with congregants because the pastor serves as the spiritual father of that congregation. To some ministers, "Sexual contact with congregants is considered spiritual incest. On the other hand, many ministers do not believe a relationship with a congregant is wrong, as long as both parties are single." [12]

---

[10] Ibid., 12.
[11] Karen Lebacqz and Ronald G. Barton, *Sex in the Parish*, 1st ed. (Louisville, KY: Westminster/J. Knox Press, 1991), 8.
[12] Ibid.

Numerous remedies and solutions have been suggested to deal with the challenge of sexuality from a human point of view, but none has really dealt with the theology of sexuality, and sexuality in the church for ministers. Lebacqz and Barton claims, "Simple aphorisms such as "Be monogamous" or "Celibacy in singleness" or "fidelity in marriage" may have their place, but they do not cover all the realities and complexities of human life, including life in the parish. In spite of all or perhaps because of the so-called sexual revolution of the 1960's, church people and leaders are not clear about roles, rules, possibilities, and limits in the sexual arena. The confusion is partly about which behaviors are acceptable. Is it permissible for the pastor who is single to date a single parishioner? What about dating other staff in the church? As long as both parties are "consenting adults," is there anything wrong? If something is wrong, what is it? Is it only adultery that makes sexual contact wrong?"[13]

It is interesting to note that Lebacqz raises some intriguing questions as it relates to the ethics of ministerial relationships, yet it appears she never gives her opinion on the matter. She never states whether she feels it is right or wrong. However, authors Marie Fortune, Dwight Hopkins and Anthony Pinn tackle the same subject matter with all three taking similar stances on the matter.

---

[13] Ibid., 8-9

Based on their writings, they all feel a relationship between a minister and congregant is wrong.[14]

In *Sexual Abuse by Clergy: A Crisis for the Church*, Marie Fortune states her position. She states, "Sexual contact by ministers and pastoral counselors with congregants/clients undercuts an otherwise effective pastoral relationship and violates the trust necessary in that relationship. It is not the sexual contact per se that is problematic but the fact that the sexual activity takes place within the pastoral relationship. When this particular boundary is violated, the relationship changes and the potential for harm increases."[15] Therefore, when it comes to professional ethics, Marie Fortune feels it is a violation for clergy to engage in any type of sexualized behavior with a congregant. Fortune also explains why she feels it is wrong for a minister to be sexual with someone he or she supervises. Below are the four reasons she provides to support her position:

First, it is a violation of role. The ministerial relationship presupposes certain role expectations. The minister/counselor is expected to make available certain resources, talents, knowledge, and expertise which will serve the best interests of the congregant, client, staff member, student intern, etc. Sexual contact is not part of the ministerial or professional role.

[14] Marie Fortune and James N. Poling, Sexual Abuse By Clergy, A Crisis For The Church (Decatur, GA: Journal of Pastoral Care Publications, 1994), 4-5.
[15] Ibid.

Second, it is a misuse of authority and power. The role of minister/counselor carries with it authority and power and the attendant responsibility to use this power to benefit the people who call upon the minister's/counselor for service. This power can easily be misused, as is the case when a professional uses, intentionally or otherwise, his or her authority to initiate or pursue sexual contact with a congregant, client, etc. Even if it is the congregant who sexualizes the relationship, it is still the minister/counselor's responsibility to maintain the boundaries of the ministerial relationship and not pursue a sexual relationship.

Third, it is taking advantage of vulnerability. The congregant, client, employee, student intern, etc. is by definition vulnerable to the minister/counselor, i.e., in multiple ways, she/he has fewer resources and less power than the minister/counselor. When the latter takes advantage of this vulnerability to gain sexual access to her or him that constitutes a violation of the mandate to protect the vulnerable from harm. The protection of the vulnerable is a practice which derives from the Jewish and Christian traditions of a hospitality code.

Fourth, it is an absence of meaningful consent. Meaningful consent to sexual activity requires a context of choice, but also mutuality and equality; hence, meaningful consent requires the absence of fear or the most subtle coercion. There is always an imbalance of power and thus inequality between the person in the ministerial role and those whom the minister/counselor supervises.

Even in the relationship between two persons who see themselves as "consenting adults," the difference in role precludes the possibility of meaningful consent.[16]

Dwight Hopkins and Anthony Pinn feel that relationships between pastors and congregants are wrong because they cannot be mutual. They are of the opinion that the pastor has the power to manipulate the other person. In the book, *Loving the Body: Black Religion Studies and the Erotic,* Dwight Hopkins and Anthony Pinn declares "Unlike sexual relationships, pastoral relationships are not mutual. Parishioners do not have the responsibility of offering guidance and leadership to ministers. Clergy disrespect God's gift of sexuality when they abuse their power through manipulation or harassment. They demean its blessedness with sexual conduct that assumes a right to violate trust and exploit vulnerability. They thwart opportunities to realize that the gift of sexuality signifies human equality and uniqueness before God."[17]

In the article, *The Abuse of Power: A View of Sexual Misconduct in a Systemic Approach to Pastoral Care,* Linda Robinson states, "When a hierarchical relationship exists, whether perceived or real, the potential for the abuse of power is present, and it is the responsibility of the one seen in authority (pastor) to be aware of this dynamic in the network of care that she or he provides. Clergy must examine the power imbalance that exists in

---

[16] Ibid., 8-9.
[17] Dwight N. Hopkins and Anthony B. Pinn, *Loving the Body: Black Religious Studies and the Erotic*, 1st ed., Black Religion, Womanist Thought, Social Justice (New York: Palgrave Macmillan, 2004), 47.

interactions with others in their congregation and their community as part of their social location as caregivers."[18] Peter Mosgofian and George Ohlschlager says in the book *Sexual Misconduct in Counseling and Ministry,* that "Those who are in position of authority in the church and professional counseling must respect the impact of their power on the lives of those they counsel, lead, and advise....Many who come to counselors and pastors for help, and some who work with pastors in ministry, are at risk for forbidden sexual entanglements because of their vulnerability and weaker position in the relationship"[19]

After reading the differing opinions of these authors, my opinion regarding the subject matter is similar. I believe a pastor should not engage in a sexual relationship with a member of his or her congregation, since it is difficult to maintain professional boundaries when trying to please personal desires. When those professional boundaries are crossed someone gets hurt emotionally as well as spiritually. In addition, if the relationship does not work out as planned, will that hinder the pastor's ability to minister to the individual? Will that person still respect you as their pastor? If both parties move on and enter into different relationships, how will the congregation view the pastor? This is not to say that a pastor cannot find a good spouse within the congregation. All

---

[18] Linda Hansen Robinson, *"The Abuse of Power: A View of Sexual Misconduct in a Systemic Approach to Pastoral Care,"* Pastoral Psychology, Vol.52, No. 5 (May 2004): 396.
[19] Peter Mosgofian and George Ohlschlager, Sexual Misconduct in Counseling and Ministry (Eugene, OR: Wipf & Stock, 1995), 24.

things are possible. However, pastors and ministers have to be very careful about all relationships; especially an intimate relationship with a member of his/her congregation.

Wolves In Sheep's Clothing

Although the pastor is always responsible for his or her actions, all cases of clergy misconduct are not instigated by the pastor. There are many cases that have been instigated by a member of the congregation. However, the pastor is still obligated as the professional, and the one in the position of power to maintain boundaries. Many pastors have failed, and ended up in some messy situations for crossing boundaries that were instigated by members.

Early on in my first pastorate a senior pastor once told me, to be careful when the women in the church are extra nice to you. When I asked him why he made that statement, he replied, "Son there are some genuine and nice women in the church, but there are also some *wolves dressed in sheep clothing.*" He said:

> Wolves dressed in sheep clothing are the women in church that every male pastor need to stay away from. There are some women in the church who will be nice to you because they really like and respect you as their pastor, but there will also be some women who lust for you because of your position of power. These women are wolves dressed in sheep clothing. These women do not respect boundaries, nor do they care about your wife. They do not care about your family, or your image in the community. They do not care who gets hurt; they are only concerned about themselves. These women will do whatever they can to get with the pastor, even if it makes them look bad. They come to church to see the pastor, not

to hear the Word of God from the pastor. They will go out of their way just to speak to the pastor, even if it means standing in a long line. Often times they will hold a conversation with the pastor "about nothing," and not speak to the 1st lady, even if she is standing right beside him. They dress in ways which are not appropriate for church, or any religious setting; just to get the pastors attention. They always need counseling or some type of help, and they never want to meet with anyone but the pastor.

The point this senior pastor was trying to get across is that we should never be fooled by a pretty face, a smile and nice gestures, because there may be some hidden motives. He pointed out that there are some genuine, loving and sincere women in the church, but there are also some wolves dressed in sheep clothing.

These are some additional lessons about Wolves in Sheep Clothing.

1) If you are married, when your wife tells you to watch "her" listen, she knows what she's talking about. They see what we do not see, or too caught up in our ego to see.

2) If they do not respect your wife, they really do not respect you.

3) Do not interact with women in the church that do not acknowledge your wife. Some women will use you to hurt her.

4) It does not matter how attractive "she" may be, a wolf is a wolf, even if she is dressed in sheep clothing.

5) Wolves do not keep secrets!

6) Wolves will destroy your character, your ministry and your family!

7) Wolves do not go away easy.

8) Wolves have no regard for boundaries.

9) Wolves are selfish, they do not care about others, or the church; they only look out for themselves.

10) Wolves cannot hurt you unless you cross the line! Stay in your lane!

11) Female pastors need to be careful also, because there are some male wolves in the congregation.

Picking Up The Pieces

CHAPTER TWO

A HISTORICAL LOOK AT CLERGY MISCONDUCT

Clergy misconduct first began receiving extensive media coverage during the late 1980s and the early 1990s in the United States. However, this is not to suggest it only became a problem during those years; clergy misconduct dates back to biblical times.

The Old Testament reports that God rejected the sons of Eli because they misused their position to engage in sexual misconduct. "These wicked men, who had no regard for the Lord"…"slept with the women who served at the entrance to the tent of meeting" (1Samuel 2:12, 22).[20] In 2 Samuel Chapter 11, David the king of Israel and Judah, who was considered to be a man after God's own heart, also committed misconduct when he had Uriah killed after learning she became pregnant due to their sexual encounter. These are just two of many incidents of misconduct by religious leaders in the bible.

Clergy misconduct has been an issue within the church for centuries, especially within the Catholic Church. History reveals the Catholic Church has faced problems of clergy misconduct as

---

[20] Stanley J. Grenz, and Roy D. Bell, *Betrayal of Trust: Confronting and Preventing Sexual Misconduct* (Grand Rapids, MI: Baker Publishing Group, 2001), 22.

far back as the second century.[21] Many traditional Catholics were under the impression that the II Vatican Council, with its liberal rules created a climate which encouraged the priest to assume the role of sexual predator.[22] However, based upon several historical facts, this view is inaccurate. Abuse and misconduct by priests was actually occurring long before the II Vatican (1962-1965). Although mandatory celibacy among Catholic Clerics did not come into existence until the twelfth century at the Second Lateran Council of 1139, a number of leaders within the Roman Catholic Church had been advocating for it since the fourth century.[23] The push for mandatory celibacy was a result of the multiple accusations of priestly misconduct. During that time many of the priests were accused of adultery, homosexuality and child abuse. The rationale behind this push stemmed from the belief that if a priest took a vow of celibacy these unethical behaviors would be controlled or significantly reduced.[24]

In 306 AD, at the Council of Elvira, nearly half of the canons passed at the convocation dealt with aberrant sexual behaviors committed by clerics. The Council of Elvira also received official documents, which revealed how strongly the church was

---

[21] Thomas P. Doyle, A. W. Richard Sipe, and Patrick J. Wall, *Sex, Priests, and Secret Codes: The Catholic Church's 2000-Year Paper Trail of Sexual Abuse* (Los Angeles: Volt Press, 2006), 295.
[22] Jim Gilbert, B*reach of Faith, Breach of Trust: The story of Lou Ann Sootiens, Father Charles Sylvestre, and Sexual Abuse within the Catholic Church* (Bloomington, IN: Universe, 2009), 1.
[23] Ibid., 2
[24] Ibid.

preoccupied with regulating the sex lives of its clergy.[25] At other times, the church had issues with clerical behavior, which was not just immoral, but reprehensible and criminal.[26] This behavior included, but was not limited to, child sexual abuse. For decades, cases of child sexual abuse surfaced in the Catholic Church, many of which were swept under a rug. Despite the dark view with which sexual abuse of children was regarded, it has continued to be a recurring problem among clergy for years.

Another source, which was used to discover misconduct by clergy during early Catholic history, was the recording of individual confessions by priests.[27] Many of which revealed the sexual crimes committed against boys and girls. Due to the number of times sex acts were documented, it became obvious the problem was not an isolated one, but rather a far-reaching issue throughout the community and church at large. Nevertheless, for a long time the church engaged in a widespread conspiracy not only to deny the existence of sexual abuse, but often deliberately provided cover for its perpetrators.[28]

In 1051, a reform-minded Benedictine monk, St. Peter Damian, attempted to write how he felt the Catholic Church of that day should deal with what he considered the increasing threat of sexual abuse by clergy. Despite the majority of these unclean acts receiving general acceptance as the norm, Damian believed it

---

[25] Doyle, Sipe, and Wall, *Sex, Priest, and Secret Codes*, 295.
[26] Ibid.
[27] Ibid., 296.
[28] Ibid.

should be stopped immediately. Therefore, he submitted a document entitled, "The Book of Gomorrah," to Pope Leo IX.[29] Damian was adamant in his belief that the church had been far too lenient on those who committed such heinous crimes and something needed to be done immediately. The reaction of Pope Leo was similar to how the Roman Catholic hierarchy had dealt with this issue over the years. After learning of the allegations, Pope Leo praised Damian for his findings. However, he did not remove the guilty clergy, but instead elected to only take action against those who were repeat offenders over a long period of time.[30]

Once again, this proved to be an unsuitable remedy. For many who were punished for their actions received a trivial punishment and were allowed to continue their priestly duties in much the same manner as they had previously done. This lack of both punishment and accountability began to take its toll on the victims, their families, and countless others who upheld the moral standards of the church. As a result, scores of reforms began to emerge against the authorities of the church. For instance, during the Fourth Lateran Council (1215) and Council of Basel (1449), reformers lashed out at church officials within the Catholic Church who allowed clerics to get away with crimes of a sexual nature.

---

[29] Gilbert, *Breach of Faith and Trust*, 3.
[30] Ibid., 4.

Both of these councils made it clear that vices among priest could not be stopped unless the superiors played an integral role.[31]

Although the Church received pressure to take decisive actions against those whom engaged in misconduct, not a lot was done. The lack of response from the hierarchy was found to be the premise to many of the revolts against the Catholic Church.

The Protestant Revolt

The Protestant revolt was a rebellion against the authorities of the Catholic Church from 1520 and 1570.[32] Abuses within the church had long been evident. For several centuries, devout churchmen spoke out against corruption and the loss of spirituality among the clergy. Clergy from the highest to the lowest of ranks frequently led immoral lives. In particular, clergy would sell church offices, including bishoprics (called simony). Another issue among clergy was the practice by which one man held several church offices (called pluralism). In addition, the church also had problems with clergy for the practice whereby powerful Church offices went to relatives of princes, bishops and popes (called nepotism).[33]

In some monasteries, monks and nuns ignored their vows of poverty and chastity and opted to live for worldly pleasure. Due to

---

[31] Ibid.
[32] Carlton J. H. Hayes, *A Political and Cultural History of Modern Europe* (New York: Published for the United States Armed Forces Institute by Macmillan, 1944), 127.
[33] Ibid.

the necessity to meet the expenses of their own costly style of living, the burden fell on the parishioners. As a result, church attendees resented the heavy expenditures of the church and its constant demand to collect money.[34] Since the early twelfth century, these abuses spawned pleas for reform in every generation. After incessant complaining regarding the lifestyles of popes, bishops, pastors, monks, and all others who abused their leadership positions, the people took action.

In one instance, the great Erasmus (1466-1536) wrote "Praise and Folly," criticizing theologians and monks. He stated, "The foolish people thought that religion consisted simply in pilgrimages, in vocation of saints, and veneration of relics."[35] Out of his desire for Christianity to regain its spiritual integrity within the church, Erasmus published in 1516 the Greek text of the New Testament with a Latin translation, with notes which challenged many theologians. This publication became the source-text for Bible translations by Martin Luther into German and by William Tyndale into English.

In the sixteenth century, a group of religious leaders, including Martin Luther, John Calvin, and Huldrych Zwingli, raised the intensity of the moment. They applied the word reformation not only to a reform in morals, but to an open break which they made with the government and doctrines of the Catholic Church.[36] The

---

[34] Ibid., 128.
[35] Ibid., 129.
[36] Ibid.

notion that believers should depend on the Bible rather than the church formed the theologians' basis for reform. The reformers learned this theology from Wycliffe and Hus. This revolt goaded the church into taking repressive action against its ministers at the Council of Trent, convened in 1545.[37] For example, the council fathers decided to abolish concubinage, which they considered to be "the supreme disgrace," and re-impose chastity on each other.[38] "While many radical reforms were adopted, the proposal which would allow priests to marry was dismissed, and mandatory celibacy was reinforced."[39]

Multiple attempts were made at the Council of Trent to create laws that would prevent a number of the unethical acts by clergy from continuing to occur. However, this council was no more successful than any other Catholic Council that preceded it. Despite passing many resolutions intended to reform various abuses in the area of papal finances, the council was unable to stop the selling of ecclesiastical offices or to prevent one individual from holding several offices. These and many other instances of misconduct concerning the ecclesiastical offices were the reasons for the drafting of Luther's Ninety-Five Theses.[40]

Martin Luther is one of the few individuals of whom it may be said that the history of the world was altered by his work. Luther's

---

[37] Ibid., 130.
[38] Timothy Mitchell, *Betrayal of the Innocents: Desire, Power, and the Catholic Church in Spain* (Philadelphia: University of Pennsylvania Press, 1998), 11.
[39] Gilbert, *Breach of Faith and Trust*, 5.
[40] Bernhard Lohse, *Martin Luther: An Introduction to His Life and Work* (Philadelphia: Fortress Press, 1986), 10.

Ninety- Five Theses ranged all the way from the complaints of the aggrieved Germans to the cries of a wrestler in the night watches. One portion demanded financial relief, the other called for the crucifixion of the self.[41] In the Ninety-Five Theses, Luther applied his evangelical theology to indulgences. He hoped thereby to find an answer to a practical problem which had disturbed him and other Christians for a long time. He attacked the sale of indulgences when he nailed the Ninety-Five Theses to the door of the Wittenberg castle. The theses challenged the notion of selling indulgences as a corrupt practice, but also as theologically unsound practices.

In the book, *Here I Stand: A Life of Martin Luther*, Bainton says, "Luther took no steps to spread his theses among the people. He was merely inviting scholars to dispute and dignitaries to define, but others surreptitiously translated the theses into German and gave them to the press. In short order they became the talk of Germany. What Karl Barth said of his own unexpected emergence as a reformer could be said of Luther, that he was like a man climbing in the darkness a winding staircase in the steeple of an ancient cathedral. In the blackness he reached out to steady himself, and his hand laid hold of a rope. He was startled to hear the clinging bell.[42] The response which Luther received from his Ninety-Five Theses was not what he had in mind when he posted

---

[41] Roland Herbert Bainton, *Here I Stand: A Life of Martin Luther* (New York: Abingdon-Cokesbury Press, 1950), 66.
[42] Ibid.

them; he meant them for the people who were concerned. However, it became the premise for the reformation of the Catholic Church.

The Counter-Reformation

Shortly after the opening of the Council of Trent, revival took place within Roman Catholicism. More specifically, the Roman Catholic Church developed a means of combating the Protestant Reformation, in order to limit its influence. They countered the Reformation by reforming itself from within in order to eliminate the grounds of the Protestant criticism. Because of the Counter Reformation, many of the abuses and issues which initiated the reform were removed.[43] For example, one concern for Protestants was *solicitantes*. *Solicitantes* is a Spanish term which describes clergy accused of using the confessional to procure sex.[44]

In their attempt to bring about a different result, the Counter Reformation designed a new confessional with a wooden grille replacing the traditional curtains to separate the priest from the one confessing.[45] The Counter Reformation was effective in many respects, but it appeared to be too little, too late. The new Protestant churches were the wave of the future; while Catholicism remains a prominent religion, in a few centuries it would cease to be the majority religion in the Western world.

---

[43] Alister E. McGrath, *Christian Theology: An Introduction*, 3rd ed. (Oxford; Malden, MA: Blackwell Publishers, 2001), 66.
[44] Mitchell, *Betrayal of the Innocents,* 2.
[45] McGrath, *Christian Theology*, 67.

The Contemporary Dilemma

It is obvious clergy misconduct was a major dilemma in the history of the modern church. However, it is not simply a historical issue, for the church is still dealing with issues of misconduct among its leaders today. Although not well recorded as a part of religious history in the United States, sexual misconduct between professionals and clients is a very old phenomenon. Yet only in the present century have efforts been made to determine the extent of this discomforting problem. Unfortunately, much of the current interest and research stems from lawsuits against various mental health professionals and clergy.[46]

However, a few studies have been conducted which give some disturbing numbers about clergy misconduct. For example, in 1984 a study was conducted which revealed, 12.67% of clergy who took a survey reported that they had sexual intercourse with a church member. This percentage is the same across lines of denomination, theological orientation, and gender. It does not compare favorably with other helping professions, as among clinical psychologists, only 5.5% of males and 0.6% of females reported sexual intercourse with clients. Thus, twice as many clergy self-report sexual intercourse with congregants as do psychologists. In addition, 75.51% of clergy in this study reported knowledge of

---

[46] Jeff T. Seat, James T. Trent, and Jwa K. Kim, "The Prevalence of Contributing Factors of Sexual Misconduct Among Southern Baptist Pastors in Six Southern States," *Journal of Pastoral Care*, (Winter, 1993), 363.

another minister who had sexual intercourse with a church member.[47]

Moreover, in *Beyond the Scandals*, Rediger says, "even though sexual misconduct is rampant in our society, its occurrence among leaders of organized religion remains scandalous, while other occurrences by inference must seem like normal life in America."[48] Because of multiple instances of clergy misconduct by well-known evangelists such as Jimmy Swaggart, Jim Baker, Oral Roberts, Bishop Anthony Jinwright, among others, came an impression that all clergy were under suspicion. Although the majority of the focus has been devoted to the Catholic Church in the United States regarding misconduct, the church at-large must still recognize that these issues implicate all clergy and organized religion. Mainline and evangelical Protestants are quietly thankful that this wave of clergy scandals is focused on the Catholic priesthood. But allegations and suspicions of misconduct continue to trouble many denominational offices and parishes.[49]

In a poll published by the *Twin Cities Star Tribune* in February of 1993, 2% of Minnesotans said they had been touched by church workers in a way which made them feel uncomfortable.[50] The epidemic of clergy misconduct in recent years has reached

---

[47] Marie Fortune and James N. Poling, Sexual Abuse by Clergy: A Crisis for the Church (Decatur, GA: Journal of Pastoral Care Publications, 1994), 5.
[48] G. Lloyd Rediger, *Beyond the Scandals: A Guide to Healthy Sexuality for Clergy*, Prisms (Minneapolis: Fortress Press, 2003), 3.
[49] Ibid., 8.
[50] Nils Friberg and Mark R. Laaser, *Before the Fall: Preventing Pastoral Sexual Abuse* (Collegeville, MN: Liturgical Press, 1998), viii.

depressing numbers. A survey conducted by Fuller Seminary in 1984 using four denominations revealed shocking and disturbing numbers about clergy misconduct. The results of the survey found 38% of clergy had sexual contact with parishioners, 12 % engaged in sexual intercourse, and 76% knew of colleagues who engaged in sexual intercourse with a church member.[51] With statistics such as these, it is obvious clergy misconduct is neither prone to one denomination nor an issue of the past. In fact, the church continues with this struggle in the twenty-first century.

Clergy Misconduct in the Black Church

No denomination or race has been fortunate enough to escape the damaging effects of clergy misconduct. For years, it was deemed a Roman Catholic issue; however, the Black Church has also had its share of clergy misconduct cases. Author J. L. King points out in his book, *On the Down Low: A Journey into the Lives of "Straight" Black Men Who Sleep with Men*, "You hear a lot of talk about Roman Catholic priests and their sexual misconduct. But no one is talking about what's going on in black churches.

The Black church has to stop the hypocrisy. Black churches condemn homosexuality, while the pastor is carrying on an affair with Sister Jeanette, who sings in the choir. If you have an extramarital affair with a sister in the church, are you any more sinful than a man who is having an affair with one of the deacons?

---

[51] Rediger, *Beyond the Scandals*, 9.

"[52] King feels the Black church condemns the sin of its members, yet ignores and covers up the misconduct of its pastors.   In   the book, *I May Not Get There With You: The true Martin Luther King Jr.*, Michael Eric Dyson says, "The failures of the black church reverberate widely because the church remains the dominate institution in black culture and the black preacher a staple in sacred and secular affairs."[53] He goes on to say, "The ability to 'tell the story' as black preachers is the most useful, and most misused, ability of black religious leaders. The gift of black preaching has been a tool used for inspiration and empowerment of blacks for years, but it has too often been used to line the pockets of materialistic ministers or cause vulnerable women to swoon and sexually submit under the hypnotic sway of eloquence. And the genius of black rhetoric has also been used to obscure personal and professional misconduct."[54]

Moreover, in many Black churches, the majority of the incidents of clergy misconduct involved male pastors. This is largely because of the demographics of the black church. The overwhelming majority of most black congregations are comprised of women. For this very reason is why Charles Eric Lincoln states, "There are great social pressures and preferences within black churches for the pastor to get married. Because of the

---

[52]J.L.King, *On The Down Low: A Journey Into The Lives Of Straight Black Men Who Sleep With Men* (Harlem: Moon Broadway, 2004), 83.
[53]Michael Eric Dyson, *I May Not Get There with You: The True Martin Luther King, Jr* (New York: Free Press, 2000), 135.
[54] Ibid., 143

predominance of female members in black churches, unattached single clergy, especially males, tend to be viewed as a threat to the stability of congregational life."[55] However, it has been proven that marriage does not prevent clergy misconduct from taking place in the black church. The majority of the scandals involving sexual misconduct involved clergy who were married.

In *Loving the Body: Black Religious Studies and the Erotic,* Dwight Hopkins and Anthony Pinn discuss incidents of clergy misconduct between women and married black ministers. In 1958, Rev. Ralph Abernathy was said to have been involved in a sexual relationship with a parishioner named Vivian Davis. When her husband, Edward Davis, found out about the affair, he came to the church office at the First Baptist Church and tried to kill Abernathy. When Edward Davis went to court, his wife testified to her natural and unnatural sexual acts with Rev. Abernathy. In turn, Edward Davis was acquitted and Rev. Abernathy was later embraced and forgiven at the Negro Civil Rights meeting led by his friend, Dr. Martin Luther King, Jr.[56]

Another prominent example involved Rev. Henry Lyons, the well-known pastor of the St. Petersburg's Bethel Metropolitan Baptist Church, who was also the president of the National Baptist Convention (NBC). In 1997, it was reported that Rev. Henry

---

[55] C. Eric Lincoln and Lawrence H. Mamiya, *The Black Church in the African-American Experience* (Durham, NC: Duke University Press, 1990), 127.
[56] Dwight N. Hopkins and Anthony B. Pinn, *Loving the Body: Black Religious Studies and the Erotic*, 1st ed., Black Religion, Womanist Thought, Social Justice (New York: Palgrave Macmillan, 2004).41.

Lyons was engaged in extramarital relationships with two women. Both women were hired to work for the Baptist Convention, in different capacities. It was also reported that Lyons had another sexual relationship with a churchgoer. Lyons' activities began receiving considerable national press because of the financial embezzlement (totaling millions of dollars) from the black Baptist denomination that was entangled with his relationships to these women. When the wife of Henry Lyons learned of her husband's relationship with Brenda Edwards, she tried to burn down the $700,000 house that her husband and Ms. Edwards purchased together apparently using church funds. The arson occurred while Rev. Lyons and Ms. Edwards were traveling together in Nigeria.

Lyons faced some opposition with the National Baptist Convention as a result of the news coverage about his financial misdeeds and extramarital relationships. After tearful pleadings for forgiveness at the NBC annual meetings, Lyons was repeatedly retained as their leader. Though he previously denied, Lyons later apologized to his wife at a board meeting in Kansas City. Again, Lyons was not asked to step down. In fact, after this apology, a love offering was collected on the convention floor for his legal expenses and he boldly announced that he would seek another five-year term. We need to develop criteria for how black churches hold their clergy accountable for sexual misconduct.[57]

In yet another case, in 1998 at the Bethel A.M.E. Church in Madison, New Jersey a woman filed a lawsuit after what happened

---

[57]Ibid., 42-43.

when she went to her minister for counseling. She went to discuss her struggle with her sexual attraction to a woman in the church. According to the woman, Rev. Donald Brown told her she needed an older man and he would help her. He also told her that she needed a triangle, with him and his wife. Offended by the statement, she filed charges of sexual harassment.[58] Although many black churches desire their pastor to be married, history has proven that marriage does not prevent clergy misconduct from taking place.

A more recent case which took place involved Bishop Anthony and Pastor Harriet Jinwright. They were the Pastors of Greater Salem Church located in Charlotte, North Carolina. On May 4, 2010 *The Charlotte Post* reported that both pastors were convicted of federal income tax evasion for failing to report more than $2.3 million in income between 2002 and 2007. The 19-count indictment alleged the couple conspired to defraud the government, evaded taxes, filed false tax returns and committed mail fraud. Anthony Jinwright, 53, was convicted on 13 counts and the charges carried a maximum of 53 years imprisonment. Harriet Jinwright, 50, was acquitted on nine of 13 counts, but still faces a maximum sentence of 20 years. Federal sentences are served without parole. The publisher of this article wrote: "This case was about tax evasion, pure and simple, said U.S. Attorney Anne Tompkins. Notwithstanding any claims to the contrary, this case

---

[58]Ibid., 43.

was not investigated or prosecuted because of the Jinwright's positions as members of the clergy. Bishop and Pastor Jinwright chose to use their positions within their church to collect enormous amounts of compensation, but ignore the tax responsibilities that all U.S. citizens must bear. That violation of well-understood federal law was the basis for this case."

According to evidence presented during the trial, the Jinwrights collected $6 million in income over a five-year period, but failed to report it on their federal taxes and failed to pay nearly $700,000. The Jinwrights countered that they didn't knowingly skirt paying taxes and were confused about whether to report money from honoraria deriving from speaking engagements. "The criminal tax laws are designed to protect the public interest in preserving the integrity of the nation's tax system," said Jeannine Hammet, special agent in charge of the IRS Criminal Investigation Division in Charlotte. "Every working person bears the responsibility to pay their own fair share of the country's tax burden.[59]

As seen above and throughout history, the Black Church has not been exempt from incidents of clergy misconduct. Just like every other institution of faith, the Black Church has also had to contend with scandals, sexual misconduct, financial improprieties, and misuse of authority from its leaders. Many people feel just like the Catholic Church, the black church needs reform as it relates to clergy misconduct because there appears to be a double standard.

---

[59] The Charlotte Post - Jinwrights convicted in federal tax case. May 4, 2010.

Picking Up The Pieces

CHAPTER THREE

THE EFFECTS OF CLERGY MISCONDUCT

The Effects on the Victims

When a member of clergy has committed some form of misconduct it creates multiple problems for the victims, their families, the church, and the minister who is to follow. The relationship a person has with the pastor/clergy person can also determine how he or she is affected by the misconduct. For instance, a person who has a close relationship with the pastor may find it hard to believe the accusations of misconduct. They may feel the victim or others in the church are attacking the pastor's character. On the other hand, someone who does not have a close relationship with the pastor may not feel any hurt feelings at all. Feelings vary based on one's relationship with the pastor.

Nils Friberg supports this theory in his book, *Restoring the Soul of a Church.* Friberg states, "When sexual misconduct occurs, the impact on different people depends on a number of variables. Three major ones are the nature of congregants' relationship to the church, to the perpetrator, and the level of fiduciary trust placed in the clergy person. This is analogous to those who have experienced bereavement, whose grief depends upon the kind of relationship they have had with the deceased. Those who are closest in relationship to the perpetrating clergy are usually hit the hardest because the ties and interrelationships are inevitably more intense. However, beyond the degree of relationship, the impact depends also on the process involved in the revelation and the way this happens over time. One's personal history will also be a factor."[60]

For some victims, clergy misconduct, especially sexual misconduct, may cause them to lose the sense that church is a safe place. Some victims of clergy misconduct stop going to church altogether. They lose trust in pastors. It has been said that some people have even lost their trust in God due to the behaviors of clergy.[61] I personally have not found anyone that has lost his or her trust in God due to clergy misconduct. However, I have heard individuals question why God would allow certain things to happen to them. It is my opinion that clergy misconduct may cause a person to lose faith in clergy, however not necessarily in God.

Clergy misconduct can also be damaging to victims' mental health. Kathryn Flynn explores this theory via her book, *The Sexual Abuse of Women by Members of the Clergy*. According to her, "Surviving sexual abuse is similar to surviving war. Survivors of both may experience trauma and consequently suffer from Post-Traumatic Stress Disorder (PTSD). This condition involves

---

[60] Nils Friberg and others, *Restoring the Soul of a Church: Healing Congregations Wounded by Clergy Sexual Misconduct* (Collegeville, MN: Liturgical Press, 1995), 55.
[61] Miles, *Pastor As Moral*, 104.

characteristic symptoms that develop in response to a psychological disturbing event. Post-Traumatic Stress Disorder is a normal and not a pathological reaction to an abnormally stressful situation. It is a human reaction to severely distressing life situations that disrupt physical and psychological equilibrium."[62]

Furthermore, not only can victims suffer from PTSD due to clergy misconduct, they can also suffer from guilt and shame. Victims who are struggling with these emotions may have a tendency to shut down and not share the pain and hurt, which has taken place in their life. For example, some victims may fail to report the misconduct out of fear for their personal safety; still others may dread being blamed. They internalize the pain and do not seek help to deal with the feelings of hurt and betrayal.

In the book, *Recovering the Lost Self: Shame –Healing for Victims of Clergy Sexual Abuse*, Elisabeth Horst explains, "Sexual abuse victims can feel like lost children. When the abuser is a member of clergy, the victim may feel lost in relation to God as well as within the human community of the church. Victims may feel vulnerable and in need of help, painfully aware of their own invisibility, especially to those in authority; and at the same time, they may feel quite reluctant to call attention to themselves, and not altogether sure they want or can use help at all."[63]

---

[62] Kathryn A. Flynn, *The Sexual Abuse of Women by Members of the Clergy* (Jefferson, NC: McFarland & Co., 2003), 28.

[63] Elisabeth A. Horst and Interfaith Sexual Trauma Institute (Collegeville, MN.), *Recovering the Lost Self: Shame-Healing for Victims of Clergy Sexual Abuse* (Collegeville, MN: Liturgical Press, 1998), 11.

The Effect on the Church

When misconduct occurs, the church's reputation can be seriously marred. The pastor's action will likely create public embarrassment, diminishing the credibility of the church throughout the community. In our increasingly litigious society, legal difficulties may be added to the long list of problems created by a pastor's misconduct.[64] Trull and Carter say, "The event of clergy misconduct polarizes the congregation. Members of the church feel shame, anger, resentment, or empathy. Some may even become vindictive. The result is usually strife and division within the congregation. Growth is stymied, attendance drops, and many families decide to join another church."[65] All of which can be detrimental to a church.

Throughout history, when clergy misconduct has occurred, it caused countless negative reactions; some of which hurt the church financially. In a parish that experienced sexual misconduct by its leader, the members demonstrated their disgust and dissatisfaction with the scandals by withholding their money. "They say they do not want their money to go to paying off victims of abusive priests."[66] During the late 1980s, a number of major ministries

---

[64] Joe E. Trull and James E. Carter, *Ministerial Ethics: Moral Formation for Church Leaders*, 2nd ed. (Grand Rapids, MI: Baker Academic, 2004), 171.
[65] Ibid., 171.
[66] William J. Bausch, *Breaking Trust: A Priest Looks at the Scandal of Sexual Abuse* (Mystic, CT: Twenty-Third Publications, 2002), 20.

suffered a significant decline resulting from clergy misconduct.[67] For instance, Oral Roberts claimed three months after his incident his ministry revenue was off $1.5 million monthly. Jimmy Swaggart reported one month after his incident he began to see a $2.5 million decline a month. Jerry Falwell reported immediately after his incident he experienced a $2 million dollar decline monthly.[68]

In extreme cases, some individuals have elected not to donate to an organization such as the Catholic Charities, simply because it has the word "Catholic" in its name.[69] Theologian Lisa Sowle Cahill is one such person, who publicly recommended withholding contributions to diocesan and Vatican organizations as a way of pressuring the hierarchy to make changes. This came at a time when the church was paying out millions of dollars in lawsuits and is still in debt.[70] To add to the financial woes for the Catholic Church, insurance companies often declined to cover the cost of the multimillion dollar lawsuits brought against the church. These, and other similar episodes, are glaring reminders that clergy misconduct of any kind drastically affects the finances of the church.[71]

The pain and disappointment felt by the people who loved and trusted their leader is yet another reaction which must be taken into

---

[67] Shupe, Stacey, and Darnell, *Bad Pastors,* 215.
[68] Ibid.
[69] Bausch, *Breaking Trust*, 20.
[70] Ibid.
[71] Ibid.

account. One writer declares, "It is like a sudden and unexpected death in the family."[72] There will be feelings of disbelief, shock, sadness, shame and disappointment when clergy misconduct has transpired. These feelings undoubtedly will also be accompanied by a myriad of questions: "How can we be sure this really happened?" "Why didn't we see this coming?" "What will come of our congregation?" "What will we tell the children?" "How can I ever trust clergy again?"[73] Unfortunately, the actions of many clergy have not only negatively affected their congregations; it also places a stain on the integrity of the office of minister.

Moreover, clergy misconduct can also affect the congregation spiritually. This is true whether it is by losing trust in clergy, losing faith in the church, questioning the providence of God, or leaving the church altogether. Friberg writes, "The spiritual impact is closely linked to the meaning of ministry and the particular denominational or congregational expectations for the involvement of ordained ministers in members' lives. For example, if the view of ministry leans more toward sacramental presence, this will mean that misconduct may powerfully affect the areas of their own spirituality involving sacraments such as baptism, Eucharist, or marriage. For those who emphasize the primacy of the Word, as historically most Protestants do, sexual misconduct might affect

---

[72] Bausch, *Breaking Trust*, 23.

[73] Nils Friberg and others, *Restoring the Soul of a Church: Healing Congregations Wounded by Clergy Sexual Misconduct* (Collegeville, MN: Liturgical Press, 1995), 58.

more strongly their receptivity and feelings about the preaching event and Scripture."[74]

This becomes one of the greatest challenges for a new pastor because one of the most effective ways to heal, encourage, and restore hope to a hurting congregation is through preaching and teaching the Word of God. Ultimately, preaching and teaching the Word of God is a vital component of the new pastor's process of rebuilding, redirecting, healing and moving the church forward. However, without the congregation's sincere receptivity of the Word of God, it could negatively affect the spiritual impact of the church and the confidence of the pastor.

When there is no receptivity of the Word of God, it becomes increasingly difficult for the new pastor/successor to reach the congregation. It also becomes difficult for the new pastor/successor to remain passionate about his or her preaching when the congregation appears they are not interested in what is being preached. Samuel Proctor says in his book, The Certain Sound of the Trumpet: Crafting a Sermon of Authority, "Without the congregation's trust in the preacher, sermons fall flat. . . When that preacher gets up to preach, no matter how incoherent the message maybe, the life lived grants it a measure of authority that no skillful outline could ever give." William Bausch shares a similar opinion about this point. In the book, *Breaking Trust: A Priest Looks at the Scandal of Sexual Abuse,* Bausch states, "When there is no trust or respect for the preacher/leader, his or her ability

---

[74] Friberg and others, *Restoring the Soul*, 55.

to reach the congregation is diminished. Every word which is spoken will be met with skepticism and doubt."[75] This is one of the sad realities which new pastors/successors will face when they follow pastors who committed some form of clergy misconduct.

The Effects of Clergy Misconduct on The "Afterpastor"

When a minister succeeds a pastor who had issues of misconduct he is usually called an "afterpastor." An afterpastor is the term a group of pastors in Minnesota called themselves after finding themselves in the same position. They followed pastors who were involved in some type of clergy-misconduct within the congregation.[76] It has been suggested that "The life of an afterpastor is relatively short, usually no more than three to five years. Afterpastors who last longer are probably in situations which one or more of the following are true: the level of betrayal was relatively slight, the congregation recognized its need for healing, good assistance was made available to the congregation, and the denomination supported the afterpastor."[77]

Many afterpastors have common experiences in relation to the challenges they faced with their congregations. Some experienced feelings of being misheard by leaders and congregants. Still others complained of being constantly criticized for no reason and treated

---

[75] William J. Bausch, *Breaking Trust: A Priest Looks at the Scandal of Sexual Abuse* (Mystic, CT: Twenty-Third Publications, 2002), 19.
[76] Friberg and others, *Restoring the Soul*, 155.
[77] Ibid.

unfairly. For example, one afterpastor described his experience this way: "I remember struggling with being so mistrusted; I wondered what I had done to earn such suspicion. I felt if I stayed any longer I would go crazy. There were many violent efforts at honest communication. I was constantly misheard. When I asked the leaders what had happened before I was called as pastor, the leadership of the congregation suddenly had amnesia. The previous senior pastor had left the church surrounded by a whirl-wind of rumors. I learned from this experience that time is no healer of betrayals of pastoral trust."[78] This example of issues the afterpastor had to contend with makes it clear that serving a wounded congregation comes with extraordinary challenges. It is also evident that time does not heal all wounds; neither does time fix unresolved issues.

"When there is public knowledge of the wounds in the congregation but no process to help the congregation heal, the pressure on the afterpastor to 'fix' the congregation can be enormous."[79] Furthermore, the challenges which come with serving as the afterpastor, along with all the other obstacles associated with pastoral ministry, may have multiple effects. The assignment can become so overwhelming it affects the afterpastor's health. It can affect the individual serving in this position by increasing stress, depression, physiological issues, and high blood pressure. "A number of afterpastors entered chemical

---

[78] Ibid., 156-157.
[79] Ibid.

dependency treatment. Others went to therapy or counseling. It was reported that one afterpastor was taken from church in an ambulance because of severe stress."[80]

In addition, the stress of leading a congregation wounded by clergy misconduct can also take a toll on the afterpastor's family. One pastor and wife shared how the challenges at church negatively affected their family. They stated, "As a family we were excruciatingly lonely and isolated, our kids made no friends. There was no energy left for them, and we had very short fuses. Upon leaving the pastorate, the eldest child in the family said bluntly, 'You're not so crabby now that we're out of that place.'[81] In another case, the afterpastor's marriage was jeopardized. The afterpastor and her husband became antagonistic and verbally violent toward each other. The children asked them often if they would make it as a family. It was an abusive, crazy, lonely time.[82] These are just a few cases of the effects of clergy misconduct on the afterpastor.

My Personal Experiences as an "Afterpastor"

Over the course of ten years I have had two different experiences serving as an afterpastor. When I arrived at my first church (New Hope) the membership was few in number, finances were tight, and the direction of the church was uncertain. However,

---

[80] Ibid., 159.
[81] Ibid.
[82] Ibid.

it was clear that this was a hurting church, trying to recover from the situation with the previous pastor. The details I received concerning what happened prior to my arrival were vague, but it was clear that healing needed to take place in this congregation. For the first year, my only focus was to bring hope, healing and stability back to the church. It appeared that some members were happy to have a new pastor, but it also felt that they were being cautious because I was a young pastor. Based on what took place prior to my arrival, they were skeptical about all pastors, especially young pastors. In the beginning of this pastorate, I felt I was being treated unfairly because of the actions of someone else. However, I did not allow that to discourage me from putting my all into this church.

I knew that the only way their perception was going to change was they had to get to know me and my family. Therefore, we began to have monthly church-wide fellowships. We traveled together, went bowling, had pot-luck dinners, hosted game nights at church, and found various ways to make church fun again. As time went on, the members got to know my family and me in a personal way, but I also got to know the various personalities of the members. Attitudes about me started changing when the members realized that I was serious about the call on my life, and I really cared about the well-being of the church. It appeared that the trust, and confidence that was lost in the position of pastor, was once again being restored. As a result the membership started significantly growing, finances increased, and a sense of joy and hope was felt in this congregation. What once was known as a place of scandal had once again become a place of love, dignity and honor.

This experience as an afterpastor came with a few challenges, but once trust was restored in the office of pastor, it made rebuilding easier. I learned from this experience that restoring trust is priority for rebuilding and moving the church forward. I also learned that trust is not automatically given, you have to earn it.

Moreover, my second experience as an afterpastor was slightly different. This experience came from my second pastorate and current church (Holy Trinity). Not knowing in the beginning that "something drastic" took place prior to my arrival, I was somewhat blindsided. I came to Holy Trinity thinking that my assignment was to rebuild a family oriented, and loving congregation, which had lost members and financial stability over time. However, after a few months I discovered the "truth." I discovered that this was a broken and hurting church, in need of healing and transformation. Once I learned all details of what took place prior to my arrival, I had to change my approach as it relates to rebuilding and moving the church forward.

Learning the truth really helped me adjust and understand the dynamics within my congregation. During my first year, there were times that I wondered "what in the world did I get myself into." Initially, I could not understand why a "family oriented church," (as I was told during the interviewing process) had so much anger and animosity toward each other. I wondered why there was so much tension between members and leaders. Also, why were there so many people who did not get along? I wondered why people were trying to isolate me, and negatively influence my opinion about other members. My first thought was somebody lied to me, because this is not a "family oriented and loving church." But when I learned the truth, I realized that it was a "family oriented and loving church," it was just a hurting "family oriented and loving church."

This revelation helped me understand that the tension, animosity, division and constant fighting, were clear signs that healing has yet to fully occur in this congregation. In addition, it became clear that if I was going to successfully rebuild and move this church forward, I had to find a way to foster healing and restore hope. The approach I took was preaching messages of hope and healing, church-wide fellowships, and showing unconditional love for the members, regardless of how I was being treated.

I must admit, this was not an easy thing to do. It is challenging to rebuild, and foster healing to a hurting congregation, when you have a few people in the congregation constantly trying to hurt and undermine you. At times it was painful and very discouraging to have people trying to damage my character, and fight against everything I did. Regardless of how good things were going, "these people" always found something to fuss and complain about. They had a problem with everything I did, and every decision I made, even though majority of the decisions I made were helping the church grow. One of my main struggles, was people were saying they loved their church, but fighting me for making the church they supposedly love better. I can honestly say there were times when ministry became so frustrating and overwhelming, that I felt like leaving and never coming back. However, in every congregation God has some Aaron's and Hur's to help you get through your tough seasons in ministry. These are the individuals who support you and hold your hands up in the midst of battle. The Bible says in Exodus 17:8-13:

> [8] The Amalekites came and attacked the Israelites at Rephidim. [9] Moses said to Joshua, "Choose some of our men and go out to fight the Amalekites. Tomorrow I will stand on top of the hill with the staff of God in my hands." [10] So Joshua fought the Amalekites as Moses had ordered, and Moses, Aaron and Hur went to the top of the hill. [11] As long as Moses held up his hands, the Israelites were winning, but whenever he lowered his hands, the Amalekites were winning. [12] When Moses' hands grew tired, they took a stone and put it under him and he sat on it. Aaron and Hur held his hands up—one on one side, one on the other—so that his hands remained steady till sunset. [13] So Joshua overcame the Amalekite army with the sword.[83]

I learned from this experience that if an afterpastor is going to be successful and not succumb to the attacks of the Amalekites (non-supportive members), he or she must have some Aaron's and Hur's on their side. It is important for every afterpastor/ pastor to have an Aaron and Hur on their side, because they will get weary

---

[83] *The New International Version.* 2011 (Ex 17:8–13). Grand Rapids, MI: Zondervan.

in this type of battle. Without support and a strong prayer life, the stress of the church could lead to a premature departure. I personally would like to thank God for my Aaron's and Hur's who supported and kept my arms lifted up, while I battled with the Amalekites within our congregation. I have truly found myself at times tired, weary and ready to walk away, but it was the support, prayers, and phone calls of my Aaron's and Hur's in my congregation that gave me the strength to keep going.

Picking Up The Pieces

CHAPTER FOUR

THE REBUILDING PROCESS

How a church responds to a situation of clergy misconduct is often a determining factor whether healing and restoration will take place. In addition, the response and approach of the afterpastor is equally important, as it relates to the rebuilding and restoration process. Beth Ann Gaede gave the most practical model to follow. In the book, *When a Congregation is Betrayed*, Gaede states, "In the aftermath of misconduct, afterpastors, taking a cue from emergency medical responders, need to understand that they cannot do everything. Rather, afterpastors must do the job of pastor, restoring trust in the person and office of minister."[84]

This is important to note because when misconduct has occurred, the trust, reputation and integrity which accompany the position is damaged. When trust in the position is damaged, it makes it harder to lead and build proper relationship with congregants. Therefore, one priority for an afterpastor should be

---

[84] Beth Ann Gaede and Candace Reed Benyei, *When a Congregation Is Betrayed: Responding to Clergy Misconduct* (Herndon, VA: Alban Institute, 2006), 53.

restoring trust in the office of minister. This is the point Gaede makes when she states, "In order to repair the damage to the office of minister, the afterpastor must do an adequate, if not better job of fulfilling the position's requirements, showing that a clergyperson can do competent work and be worthy of the trust previously betrayed. Restoring trust cannot be done by simply calling or installing a pastor of impeccable character or reputation. In order to accomplish this challenging task, the minister must provide high-quality pastoral ministry, which in straightforward terms, means doing the basic job well and faithfully fulfilling the requirements of the position with integrity and honesty. This will prove that a clergyperson can do competent work and be worthy of trust."[85]

Despite being simplistic in nature, this principle is definitely a case of easier said than done. This type of ministry task will not be easy; however, the afterpastor must do everything possible to demonstrate and cultivate trust. Simple gestures like being prompt to all obligations, maintaining good communication and being consistent in word and deed confirms the afterpastor's trustworthiness in a concrete and significant way. This will help congregations re-experience trustworthiness.[86]

It is also important that afterpastors be clear and cautious about maintaining appropriate boundaries in the role of minister/pastor.

---

[85] Ibid.
[86] Ibid.

"When boundaries are not maintained, it opens the door for failure to come in."[87] Building relationships and getting to know the people is an important step in the rebuilding process, however, the afterpastor must be careful about getting too close too fast. If the former pastor committed some form of sexual misconduct, the afterpastor will be watched closely when communicating or interacting with members, especially members of the opposite sex. This is not always an attack on the afterpastor, sometimes it's a lack of trust towards some of the women/men of the church. Therefore, the afterpastor should take his/her time to interact and get to know the members, but keeping boundaries is very important.

During both of my pastorates, when I discovered that some form of misconduct had taken place, I immediately set up boundaries which would help build confidence in the membership. For example, I informed the congregation during a business meeting that I would not meet or counsel female congregants in my office alone. I also put a procedure in place that I would not visit anyone's home without a deacon or deaconess. I do not ride female congregants in my car alone. When I shake hands after service I make sure my wife or a deacon is close, and I do not spend too much time talking with one individual. These are practices I put in place from the outset to protect myself and to build confidence in the membership. Some people may not agree with these procedures, however, it is better to be safe than sorry.

---

[87]Ibid.

One thing the afterpastor must take into consideration is that he/she cannot stop all rumors from being spread. Regardless of how hard you try to maintain boundaries and interact with integrity, somebody will accuse you of something. For a man, if you smile and hold conversations with the women in the church they will say you are flirting, but if you do not smile and talk with the women they will probably say you are gay. If you spend a lot of time with your members they will say you too close, but if you do not spend a lot of time with them they will say you distant or not personable. If you married and your spouse drives a separate car to church, they will say you having problems at home. If you start wearing nice clothes somebody will say you stealing church money. Regardless of what the afterpastor does, he or she should always expect some type of rumors to be spread. Therefore, do not allow rumors to frustrate you, it comes with the position. Just do not allow the rumors to become true.

Furthermore, if the afterpastor is going to be successful in the rebuilding and restoration process he or she must have a clear plan. Trying to rebuild a church that has been wounded by clergy misconduct without a plan or some helpful strategies, could eventually prove to be disastrous for the afterpastor, his or her family and the congregation. When I discovered the pain and condition of the church, my first plan of action was to love the people and create an environment of unity and fruitful fellowship. There were many things in the church that I wanted to change or adjust; however, those things had to be put on hold. I spent the first few months loving and trying to unify the congregation. Ultimately my goal was to make church "fun" again. My plan was to help the people heal and regain hope concerning the future of the church.

This was done through positive and encouraging preaching, church wide fellowships, and discipleship campaigns (A discipleship campaign was a contest to see who would invite the most people to church). This created some excitement and new energy within the church. One member told me that "It had been a long time since she had invited someone to the church." When I asked why she stated, "Because it was too much negative stuff going on." This conversation taught me that it is important for the afterpastor to find ways to get the members excited about the new direction of the church. When members get excited about their church, they invite others to attend, and the church grows. When the church which has experience loss begins to grow, hope is restored. When hope is restored the afterpastor gains the confidence of the members and eventually will be able to cast vision and lead the people in a new direction. But without a clear plan none of this will happen.

Overall, when the basic job is done well, it brings about a unique and essential step in healing the congregation, and thus creates the possibility that in the long term full healing will occur. Restoring hope and trust to a hurting congregation will not be an easy task for the afterpastor. Some afterpastors may never restore or earn the trust of the congregation. What is clear is that restoring trust does not just happen; it takes time and skill. Knowledgeable of the challenges to restoring trust, Gaede offers some practical steps for afterpastors to follow to assist with the process. She shares, "Afterpastors make reparations to the office of minister by exercising emotional neutrality, establishing clear boundaries, and rebuilding trust in pastoral relationships. Afterpastors who conduct their business and interact with others in ways that consistently instill confidence, display predictability, connote truthfulness, and evidence authenticity will restore to the office respect and worth, and accord to themselves the support and resources needed for greater effectiveness."[88]

Finally, afterpastors can accomplish this task of rebuilding and restoring trust by not inflicting further harm on the congregation, individuals, or the office of minister. They should foster healing to individuals and for the congregation as long as doing so does not jeopardize the afterpastor's priority, which is healing the office of minister. Afterpastors also restore trust and appropriate expectations to the office of ministry by arranging their life and work so that both personal and professional needs are appropriately fulfilled.[89]

---

[88] Ibid., 57.
[89] Ibid., 61-62.

Pastors as Models and Peace Makers

In addition to restoring trust in the office of minister and hope in the congregation, many times the afterpastor also has to serve as peacemaker. There were times in my current church when I wondered if I was a pastor, a fireman or a referee. My first few months at the church, it seemed like all I did was break up fights and put out fires. This can be overwhelming for a new pastor who is trying to adjust to a new church and new environment. One thing I have discovered in both of my pastorates is that in the aftermath of clergy misconduct, conflict within the congregation is inevitable. A lot of the conflict comes from those who support their pastor and those who want the pastor gone. Instead of congregations coming together to work through the challenges, many congregations become divided. Some congregations become divided over how the situation was handled. Others become divided based on whose side they are on. The bottom line is when clergy misconduct has occurred in the church the afterpastors will have to resolve some conflict. Therefore, the afterpastor must also become a peacemaker.

In the book, *The Peacemaking Pastor*, Alfred Poirier says, "As pastors and leaders of the church, it is our job to be like Jesus, peacemakers."[90] Jesus said, "Blessed are the peacemakers, for they will be called children of God" (Matthew 5:9). The foundation upon which all biblical peacemaking efforts rest is in the

---

[90] Alfred Poirier, *The Peacemaking Pastor: A Biblical Guide to Resolving Church Conflict*, (Grand Rapids, MI: Baker Books, 2006), 21.

understanding that God has made peace through the blood of the cross. This act of God is the only vehicle for all human reconciliation with God and peace among people.[91] It is not simply the removal of conflict from our lives and congregations. It should also be remembered that one of the main goals of peacemaking is a call to spiritual warfare, strengthening in crisis, and emancipation from evil. Its goal is to eliminate the unbearable tensions, which cripple and hurt members of the congregation.

To be effective in peacemaking, the afterpastor must develop the proper attitude. In the book, *Surviving Church Conflict*, Peters provides some guidelines for attitudes, which he feels each pastor must possess in order to be effective as a peacemaker:

> 1. The pastoral peacemaker must create a safe climate in the church for honest exchange of feelings. The pastor must reduce the fear of different groups in the church, fear that they might be excluded.

> 2. The pastoral peacemakers must learn personally the loving acceptance and forgiveness of God in one's own daily life. In addition, there must be a plan to establish congregational direction toward specific goals of cohesiveness.

> 3. The pastoral peacemaker must spend much time with appointed leadership. The pastor must continuously be involved in the healing of hurting leaders in the congregation. The pastor must also demonstrate God's love by ministering to the entire church family, without showing favoritism.

---

[91] Peters. P.45

4. The pastoral peacemaker must learn to live above the petty squabbles in church. The pastor must be assertive in love and thus be an example for the entire congregation. It is also important to keep oneself physically fit. This will help in keeping attitudes positive in times of tension.

5. The pastoral peacemaker must learn to listen with a prayerful attitude. The pastor must develop the skill in perceiving when it is beneficial to move quickly in making changes, and when it is necessary to move slowly. Members in some churches will not be emotionally ready to advance in the mission of the church. The peacemaker must always listen before acting.

If a pastor, as stated by Peters, can develop these kinds of attitudes and patterns of action it will assist and advance conflict resolution within the church."[92] When a church has experienced clergy misconduct and the members are divided, conflict resolution is a must. It will benefit not only the church, but also the sanity of the afterpastor.

Forgiveness: The Foundation for Healing and Restoration

A major part of resolving church conflict and moving a hurting church forward is involved in the process of forgiveness. Forgiveness is a term, which has the basic concept of release from bondage, the remission of debt, guilt or punishment.[93] The bible understands forgiveness as a process, which includes both the

---

[92] Ibid.P.47-48
[93] Geiko Müller-Fahrenholz, *The Art of Forgiveness : Theological Reflections on Healing and Reconciliation* (Geneva: WCC Publications, 1997). P.4

perpetrator and the victim. It can occur when the perpetrator asks for forgiveness and the victim grants it. Both sides can change through this encounter, and it can lead to the healing and restoration of formerly conflicting individuals. This can be clearly seen in Jesus' prayer from the cross: "Father, forgive them, for they do not know what they are doing" (Luke 23:34). "Forgiveness is more than a word or gesture; it is a genuine process of encounter, of healing, of releasing of new options for the future. A guilty and painful past is redeemed in order to establish reliable foundations for renewed fellowship in dignity and trust. Forgiveness frees the future from the haunting legacies of the past."[94]

Moreover, forgiveness for Christians is not a choice it is a God given command. The bible is clear when it talks about forgiveness. It says, "Be kind and compassionate to one another, forgiving each other, just as in Christ God forgave you" (Ephesians 4:32). Mark 11:25 says, "And when you stand praying, if you hold anything against anyone, forgive them, so that your Father in heaven may forgive you your sins." Matthew 6:14-15 NIV says, "For if you forgive men when they sin against you, your heavenly Father will also forgive you. But if you do not forgive men their sins, your Father will not forgive your sins." Not only are we instructed to forgive, we are also told to be ready to forgive over and over again. Matthew 18: 21-22 NIV says, "Then Peter came to Jesus and

---

[94] Ibid. P.5

asked, "Lord, how many times shall I forgive my brother when he sins against me? Up to seven times? Jesus answered, I tell you, not seven times, but seventy-seven times." We must all remember that forgiveness is a command by God, not a choice from God.

Although it has been commanded by God, forgiving others is not an easy thing to do. It is extremely hard to forgive someone who has hurt you. Not only is forgiveness a hard thing to do, it seems unfair to the victims. Dr. Terry Thomas shares in his book *Becoming A Fruit Bearing Disciple,* "For many, forgiveness seems so unfair because behind every act of forgiveness lies a wound of betrayal, and the pain of being betrayed does not fade easily away."[95] For many, forgiveness may seem unfair and impossible, but it is what we as Christian are supposed to do. We must understand it is impossible to truly forgive others in your own strength when they have hurt and betrayed your trust. Unless your heart is cleansed and changed by God, the memories and feelings will start lurking in the background, poisoning your thoughts and words. The only way to overcome these barriers is to be honest with yourself and allow the Holy Spirit to change your heart.

Afterpastors who are attempting to rebuild a hurting congregation, teaching biblical principles on forgiveness are a must. It will be a major factor in being able to move the church toward healing and restoration. Alfred Poirier says, "In any type of peace-making process, such as negotiation, mediation, or church

---

[95] Terry Thomas, *Becoming A Fruit-Bearing Disciple*, (Raleigh, NC: Voice of Rehoboth Publushing, 2005). P.88

discipline, godly forgiveness must be continually taught and practiced, because it is absolutely crucial for the true and lasting reconciliation between conflicting parties."[96]

In addition to the afterpastor preaching and teaching biblical principles of forgiveness, he or she must visibly show the congregation what forgiveness looks like. This was the case in my own context as an afterpastor. Near the end of my first year in my current context, many hurtful and evil things were said and done to me publicly and privately. Although there were many times I left church hurt, frustrated and nearly in tears, I understood that my response was important. My response could either help me or hurt me in ministry. For example, if I would have retaliated or responded to the negativity in the same way then I would have possibly lost the respect of many members. Also, I would have lost my ability to influence others. How could I teach and challenge people to do something I am not willing to do myself. Therefore, regardless how hurt and upset I was, I knew the right thing for me to do was to respond like Jesus and forgive my persecutors.

I must admit, that was a trying time for me as a new pastor/afterpastor, but my ability to forgive and be the "bigger person" helped me gain the confidence and respect of many members. It also showed the congregation that I was a pastor that practiced what I preached. A lesson that I learned during this process is that we (pastors) are not judged by what people do to us,

---

[96]Poirier. P.140

we are judge by our response. Additionally, if we are going to be successful rebuilding a hurting congregation we must preach, teach and extend forgiveness in all circumstances.

Picking Up The Pieces

CHAPTER FIVE

A BIBLICAL APPROACH TO REBUILDING

Nehemiah 2:17-18

A thorough exegetical study of the book of Nehemiah, with special emphasis devoted to chapter 2:17-18, will be used as a Biblical guide for modern readers and leaders on how to rebuild a hurting and broken community. Churches, in and of themselves are communities, for they each possess their own culture, nuances and traditions. With that in mind, the term "broken community" is also symbolic of a hurting congregation. For in both instances, effective leadership is a key component if the community or congregation is to be successful in rebuilding.

The book of Nehemiah tells the story of an exceptional leader who collaborates with others to rebuild the walls surrounding Jerusalem. He also restores the spiritual condition of God's people in the midst of perilous times. The historical setting for the book of Nehemiah dates back to around 587- 586 BC. This was the end of King Zedekiah's reign. During his reign, Zedekiah rebelled against

King Nebuchadnezzar, refusing to turn to the Lord despite many warnings from the prophets. Due to the misconduct and decisions of King Zedekiah, Nebuchadnezzar's army came (under God's direction) and destroyed Judah's independence. During this invasion, many of the residents in Judah were killed. Their valuables were taken from their homes and the temple. The building was burned and reduced to rubble. The city walls were torn down. Those who escaped death were taken into Babylonian captivity where they stayed until Babylon's fall to the Persian Empire.

The actions of King Zedekiah towards Nebuchadnezzar and his unethical behavior against God caused a disaster in the lives of the people of Judah. They were ultimately left broken and in a state of hopelessness. Similarly, countless congregations have also suffered strife and wound up hurt and bitter as a result of the actions and unethical behaviors of clergy. Throughout history, the immoral and unethical actions of clergy, kings and leaders have left congregations and communities hurt and in a state of despair. In Nehemiah's day, the people of Judah ended up in Babylonian captivity.

The fate of Judah changed in 539 BC, when King Cyrus and the Persian Empire conquered Babylon, freed the people who had been taken into exile, and allowed them to return to their homeland.[97] As there had been three deportations from the land of

---

[97] Ibid.

Judah into captivity in Babylon, the captives were set free and returned to Judah in three groups.[98]

In 538 BC, the first group returned to Judah under the leadership of Zerubbabel. In 458 BC, the second group of Jews returned, led by Ezra. Upon his return, Ezra discovered the people required reformation; they needed to return to their covenant obligations. In 444 BC, fourteen years after Ezra's return to Jerusalem, Nehemiah returned. God used Nehemiah to guide Judah in rebuilding the city's walls and reordering the people's social and economic lives.[99]

The book of Nehemiah continues the story began in the book of Ezra. When Nehemiah arrives in Jerusalem the citizens have rebuilt the temple, and the people have been restructured as a worshipping community. Yet, the people of Judah still needed a safe place where they could carry out their daily functions as a community.[100] This was a dangerous time for people of Jewish descent. For nearly a century and a half, the walls of Jerusalem lay in ruins. These very concerns were possibly what prompted Hanani, Nehemiah's brother, and other men from Judah to enlist Nehemiah's help. These men understood that perilous times call for great leaders.

---

[98] John F. Walvoord, Roy B. Zuck, and Dallas Theological Seminary., *The Bible Knowledge Commentary: An Exposition of the Scriptures*, 2 vols. (Wheaton, IL: Victor Books, 1983), 675.
[99] Ibid., 676.
[100] Noss and Thomas, *The Handbook*, 225.

This is also the case for many churches. After a congregation has suffered clergy misconduct and a major disaster, it needs a strong leader to lead them in the rebuilding process. A leader with enough influence and integrity to restore a sense of hope in the people, as well as deal with the opposition, which he/she will face during the rebuilding process. In today's society this would be the afterpastor. To the people of Judah, this is the type of leader Nehemiah was; a leader who cared about the condition of the people.

As cupbearer, Nehemiah occupied a position of immense influence within the Empire due to his closeness to the king. The position Nehemiah held was one of great trust since it was the cupbearer's responsibility to taste the wine to obviate any attempt at poisoning the king. Hence, he was in the perfect position to lay the petitions of his Jewish brethren before the highest authority. The embassy that came to him from Judah came knowing it would have a natural access to Nehemiah's sympathy, and that he in turn had access to the monarch.[101]

In this instance, Nehemiah was likened to the patriarch Joseph, who rose to high estate in the service of a foreign king. His response to the news demonstrates he was committed to his kingdom duties without compromising his Jewish identity. Nehemiah described the report that was given to him by a delegation of people from Jerusalem. This report immediately

---

[101] McConville, *Ezra, Nehemiah, Esther*, 74.

caused him distress for it contained information regarding the condition of his people and their land. Similar to a good shepherd, Nehemiah cared about the well-being of his people and was thus greatly disturbed to hear of their misfortunes. He also understood the significance of the wall.

The walls around Jerusalem were particularly vital to ensure the safety of the Jewish people. Therefore, with the walls down, the Jewish community continued to lie unprotected from the attacks and influence of its enemies. Unless action was taken, the ruined walls would be a symbol of what would happen to the people who lived in this community. In addition, the absence of walls mean the city would be virtually defenseless. The temple could be destroyed easily by the enemies because no proper stand could be made against enemies without a defense wall.[102]

Furthermore, the wall itself was more than a source of protection for Jerusalem and its citizens; it also guarded against any mixing with foreigners. Its conditions at that time were symbolic of the low esteem in which the Jews were held by its neighbors.[103] To Nehemiah, it was a disgrace for Jerusalem, God's chosen city, to lie in ruins. After all, this was the place that God had chosen to put His name. Yet, Nehemiah understood that neither the reproach nor shame would be removed until the walls were rebuilt.

---

[102] F. Charles Fensham, *The Books of Ezra and Nehemiah*, New International Commentary on the Old Testament (Grand Rapids, MI: Eerdmans, 1982), 152.
[103] Jacob Martin Myers, *Ezra. Nehemiah*, [1st ed., The Anchor Bible, (Garden City, NY: Doubleday, 1965), 105.

Likewise, when a church has suffered clergy misconduct, it is similar to the walls being down and in ruins. It brings shame and humiliation to the members of the congregation. The place that carries the name of God has become a place of scandal. This causes many members of the congregation to leave or lose hope in the church. The shame and embarrassment will not be removed until the church has been rebuilt, and trust has been restored in the office of clergy. The afterpastor must not only rebuild the church, he/she must also restore trust in the office of minister so the wall of integrity will stand again in the church and community. When Nehemiah learned of the condition of his people and his homeland, his first impulse was to turn to God in prayer, despite having the ear of and access to the king.

Nehemiah's prayer drew heavily upon Israel's rich liturgical tradition, with a strong focus on the God of heaven. In prayer, Nehemiah confesses of both personal and national sin. Only then does he turn to a summary of God's covenant promises as a basis for his twofold petition, in general for restoration of his people's fortunes and in particular for the right approach to the king.[104]

After fasting and praying, the scene shifts to Nehemiah's moment with the king. Nearly four months passed before Nehemiah's opportunity to approach the king came.

---

[104] D. A. Carson, *New Bible Commentary: 21st Century Edition*, 4th ed. (Leicester, England; Downers Grove, IL, USA: Inter-Varsity Press, 1994), 337.

The approach to the king is made in March-April, which is Nisan, the first month in the Babylonian calendar. The delay can be explained by the king's absence in Babylon during the winter months, or there may have been several royal butlers serving on a Rota system.[105] Nehemiah waited for the perfect time to make his supplication to the king.

At the time when Nehemiah attempts to proposition the king, there may have been a banquet called *tukta* during which it was considered *de rigueur* for the king to grant any request addressed to him. Or it could have been an occasion when one of the king's favorite harem women would be present.[106]

As Nehemiah continued to perform his normal duties, the king noticed a difference in Nehemiah's countenance. His emotions were obvious on his face. This was a risky time for Nehemiah because court etiquette required a cheerful and pleasant demeanor. Any hint of glumness could arouse suspicion and begin intrigue.[107] "A servant was never to let his negative emotions show before the king, for it might suggest dissatisfaction with the king. To do so might jeopardize his position or even his life. In addition, Nehemiah knew his request was a bold one. A few years earlier,

---

[105] Joseph Blenkinsopp, *Ezra-Nehemiah: A Commentary*, 1st ed., The Old Testament Library (Philadelphia: Westminster Press, 1988), 213.
[106] Ibid., 214.
[107] Ibid., 215.

this king had stopped the rebuilding of Jerusalem and now Nehemiah was going to ask that the order be reversed."[108]

Therefore, the condition of Jerusalem, along with the anxiety to secure favor from his royal master, made it such a burden that he could not carry it in concealment.[109] Curious about Nehemiah's countenance, the king inquires about the look on his face. Although fearful of the risk involved, Nehemiah does not allow his fears to destroy his opportunity to make a difference and when asked about his sadness boldly states his case. When responding to the king, Nehemiah chose his words with care and went directly to the heart of the matter.[110] "Why should my face not look sad when the city where my fathers are buried lies in ruins, and its gates have been destroyed by fire?"[111] This is a shameful and unacceptable situation for Nehemiah. It also demonstrated his great respect for his ancestors and the condition of his homeland.

Nehemiah's response clearly touched the heart of the king for he immediately asks what he could do to help the situation. As was his normal practice, Nehemiah prayed before acting or speaking. Then he requested the king's permission to travel to Judah to

---

[108] Walvoord, Zuck, and Dallas Theological Seminary, *The Bible Knowledge,* 678.

[109] Loring W. Batten, *A Critical and Exegetical Commentary on the Books of Ezra and Nehemiah*, The International Critical Commentary on the Holy Scriptures of the Old and New Testaments (New York: Scribner, 1913), 191.

[110] Johanna W. H. Van Wijk-Bos, *Ezra, Nehemiah, and Esther*, 1st ed., Westminster Bible Companion (Louisville, KY: Westminster John Knox Press, 1998), 55.

[111] International Bible Society, *Vox Dei: Holy Bible, New International Version* (Colorado Springs, CO: International Bible Society, 1993), Nehemiah 2:3.

rebuild the city where his ancestors were buried. After a short dialogue, the king grants Nehemiah his consent along with the resources needed to begin rebuilding the walls and the lives of his people.

Upon his arrival in Jerusalem, Nehemiah realized before he could reveal his intentions, he must do some research and planning. Given the potential opposition he stood to face, Nehemiah was cautious not to let information about his plan get into the wrong hands. Therefore, he did the majority of his observations at night. Having surveyed the extent of the damage and being satisfied that he had developed a feasible plan, Nehemiah revealed to the Jews why he was in Jerusalem. According to the text, there was no discussion on the matter. "Once again we need to realize that the issue is one of spiritual contention. A democratic spirit is not what the moment requires. Nehemiah proceeds rather from his conviction that the project is of God and the current state of Jerusalem is incompatible with their state as God's people."[112]

An afterpastor arriving at a church which has experienced clergy misconduct should follow Nehemiah's example in surveying the extent of the damage prior to developing a plan of action. In many cases, not everything about the incident will be disclosed during the interviewing process. It is critical to obtain as much information as possible about the situation before trying to

---

[112] McConville, *Ezra, Nehemiah, Esther*, 85.

rebuild and move the congregation forward. Once enough information has been gathered, then the planning and implementation of the rebuilding project should take place.

Such was case with Nehemiah. With all the preliminary work complete, Nehemiah motivated the people to rebuild the walls which had been destroyed. In Neh. 2:17, (New International Version) he proclaimed to the Jews, "You see the trouble we are in: Jerusalem lies in ruins, and its gates have been burned with fire. Come, let us rebuild the wall of Jerusalem, and we will no longer be in disgrace." Two essential things took place in this verse. First, he challenged them to observe the condition they were in. He then dared them to rebuild so they would no longer be in their present circumstance.

The first challenge was for them to take notice of their deplorable circumstances, which had brought them trouble and disgrace.[113] It is interesting Nehemiah used the same two words seen in chapter 1 verse 3, "trouble and shame" (Revised Standard Version). When Nehemiah used trouble, he characterized their situation by using a word that has the connotation of evil.[114] The word he used to express shame alludes to disgrace. It was a reminder of the punishment Israel received in the exile that humiliated her before other nations.[115] It was also an appeal to their

---

[113] Walvoord, Zuck, and Dallas Theological Seminary, *The Bible Knowledge*, 684.
[114] Noss and Thomas, *The Handbook*, 291.
[115] Ibid.

national and spiritual heritage. The critical issues were not safety and security, but honor and respect. The shambles of Jerusalem reflected badly upon their religious faith.[116] However, he selected his words carefully in order to achieve the maximum effect on his audience.[117]

In chapter 2, verse 17 Nehemiah implored the people to look at their present condition and come together to change it. With that in mind, Nehemiah identified himself with the people and their needs, which is a good measure for any leader attempting to motivate people to rebuild. In any community or congregation, people must believe that those attempting to lead are also a part of their family, not an outsider. A leader faces less resistance when the people feel the one in command is also one of them. In the book, *Hand Me Another Brick*, by Charles R. Swindoll, he points out:

> For Nehemiah to motivate the city planning commission and potential employees, he had to identify himself with the need. Imagine the kind of response he would have received if he said you folks have gotten yourselves into a bad mess. You know what you need to do? You need to rebuild that wall. If you need me, I'll be in my office. After all, I wasn't part of the problem. You people will have to get with it and do the work! When you cast blame and criticism, you squelch motivation. When you identify with the problem, you encourage motivation.[118]

[116] Knute Larson, Kathy Dahlen, and Max E. Anders, *Ezra, Nehemiah, Esther*, Holman Old Testament Commentary V. 9. (Nashville, TN: Broadman & Holman, 2005), 149.
[117] Fensham, *The Books of Ez-Ne*, 167.
[118] Charles R. Swindoll, *Hand Me Another Brick*, Rev. and expanded ed. (Nashville, TN: Word Pub., 1998), 56.

When Nehemiah says, "Come, let us rebuild the wall of Jerusalem, and we will no longer be in disgrace" (Neh. 2:17 NIV), he called his listeners to action, and invited them to join him in ending their state of disgrace and humiliation."[119] Those steps, which were taken by Nehemiah in this rebuilding project can serve as a blueprint for others who wish to rebuild a broken community. Breneman describes the four steps as follows:

> Nehemiah was able to discern the proper time to present the building project, and he knew how to motivate the leaders and the people. He used four incentives. (1) He identified with the people; he spoke of the trouble we are in. (2) He stressed the seriousness of the situation. A leader must be realistic and honestly assess the facts. People will have confidence in such a leader. (3) Nehemiah was committed to taking definite action. (4) He used his personal testimony of God's grace to assure them of God's favor on the project. A Christian leader must encourage trust in God by leading in faith as well as in action.[120]

Moreover, part of the task for Nehemiah was to share his vision with the community and motivate the people to work together to change the situation. Right from the start, Nehemiah made it clear he had no desire to create more trouble for them by acting without permission. He let them know he was sent by God, meaning he was religiously motivated. "I also told them about the gracious

---

[119] Noss and Thomas, *The Handbook*, 291.

[120] Mervin Breneman, *Ezra, Nehemiah, Esther*, The New American Commentary V. 10 (Nashville, TN: Broadman & Holman Publishers, 1993), 182.

hand of my God upon me and what the king had said to me." (Neh. 2:18, NIV). In order to gain the favorable regard of the people, Nehemiah informed them of how God had led him and made this all possible. "I told them of how the hand of my God had graciously provided for me, and arranged my journey to Jerusalem; and the king's words that he had spoken to me with respect to the building of the wall."[121]

Particularly then, it was vital for the people to know the favor of God was on Nehemiah as he started them on this rebuilding process. It was also important for them to recognize he has the permission of Artaxerxes to rebuild the wall. This let the people know they could join in the purposes of God, and they would have nothing to fear from the Persian government.[122] Likewise, it also gave Nehemiah double authority, which was almost impossible for the people to oppose.[123] E.G. White says in her book, *Restoring the Breach*, that "although Nehemiah bore a royal commission requiring the inhabitants to cooperate with him in rebuilding the walls of the city, he chose not to depend upon the mere exercise of authority. He sought rather to gain the confidence and sympathy of the people, well knowing that a union of hearts as well as hands

---

[121] Carl Friedrich Keil and Franz Delitzsch, *Biblical Commentary on the Old Testament* (Grand Rapids, MI: Eerdmans, 1866), Vol.4 P.110.
[122] Larson, Dahlen, and Anders, *Ezra, Nehemiah, Esther*, 149.
[123] Fensham, *The Books of Ez-Ne*, 167.

was essential to success in the great work which he had undertaken."[124]

The leadership of Nehemiah inspired the people, and gave them a sense of hope that their land and their lives could be revived. In response to Nehemiah's actions, the people declared, "Let us start rebuilding. So they began this good work" (Neh. 2:18, NIV). The unanimous response of the people confirmed Nehemiah was indeed on the right path. The people responded with a readiness, which is perhaps surprising, given that Nehemiah was a stranger in those parts. Their eagerness is a measure of the truth of what Nehemiah said. The people are instantly convinced that it is right to build the wall and the moment has come to do it.

The work had begun, and hope was restored in the people, because a leader named Nehemiah motivated them to come together and change their present condition. It takes both the hands of leadership and the hands of partnership to accomplish the work of the Lord. Warren Wiersbe says, "Leaders cannot do the job by themselves, and workers cannot accomplish much without leadership."[125] The assignment of the afterpastor is very similar in nature to Nehemiah's, namely to restore hope in a hurting congregation and motivate the people to come together and rebuild what once laid in ruins as a result of clergy misconduct.

---

[124] E.G. White, *Restoring the Breach* (Brushton, NY: Teach Services, Inc., 1997), 19.
[125] Warren W. Wiersbe, *Be Determined* (Wheaton, IL: Victor Books, 1996), 32.

Titus 2:7-8

The Nehemiah text deals with approach of the afterpastor in the rebuilding process. Titus helps the reader understand the actions and integrity of the afterpastor in the rebuilding process. Both of which are very important when rebuilding a church that has been wounded by clergy misconduct.

In Titus 2:7-8 (New International Version) Paul states, "In everything set them an example by doing what is good. In your teaching show integrity, seriousness and soundness of speech that cannot be condemned, so that those who oppose you may be ashamed because they have nothing bad to say about us." To achieve a better understanding of these two verses, the reader must have a clear knowledge of the context in which it was written.

The book of Titus, along with 1 and 2 Timothy, is known in Christian tradition as a pastoral letter or epistle. The pastoral epistles were given this title by Aquinas in the thirteenth century, then in modern times by the German scholar, Paul Anton, in the first half of the eighteenth century.[126] These letters have been grouped together primarily due to their commonality. They all largely focus on the pastor's duties in the church, and they are all addressed to individuals rather than churches.[127]

---

[126] J. L. Houlden, *The Pastoral Epistles: I and II Timothy, Titus*, Tpi New Testament Commentaries (London; Philadelphia: SCM Press; Trinity Press International, 1989), 15.
[127] Ibid., 16.

In addition, all of the epistles instruct the recipients how they should care for and organize the flock of God. They also instruct pastors how to behave in the household of God. Those instructions are very important for every pastor to adhere to, especially those whom are called to a church which has experienced clergy misconduct. When a church has been hurt due to the misconduct of its leader, the actions and integrity of the successor will be under a lot of scrutiny until proven otherwise. Therefore, it is very important for pastors, whom are called to a situation where the behavior of the previous leader has been unethical, to embrace the certain modes of behavior which are written in these Epistles.

The authenticity of Paul's authorship of the Pastoral Epistles has been a debate for centuries. Since the early nineteenth century, scholars have generated an extensive list of arguments concerning the authenticity of Paul as author of the Pastoral Epistles. Many scholars consider them not authored by Paul, but feel they are pseudonymous.[128] Most who advocate pseudonymity feel that an admirer of Paul penned the letters at a time after Paul's death and used the name of Paul in order to get acceptance of his ideas.[129] However, there has yet to be a satisfactory explanation for the

---

[128] Gordon D. Fee, *1 and 2 Timothy, Titus*, 1st ed., A Good News Commentary (San Francisco: Harper & Row, 1984), 3.
[129] Thomas D. Lea and Hayne P. Griffin, *1, 2 Timothy, Titus*, The New American Commentary V. 34 (Nashville, TN: Broadman Press, 1992), 23.

composition of the Pastorals from the point of view of pseudonymity authorship.[130]

The letter written to Titus is the shortest of the three Pastoral Epistles. In this letter, Paul writes to Titus giving him various instructions on how to provide effective leadership to the churches in Crete. Titus is called upon to deal with some challenges and set things in order in the church communities on the Island of Crete. The people in Crete are not an easy group of people to deal with, and Titus would need an extraordinary amount of love and patience to lead this church. This church needs a lot of teaching and structure.[131] Since the churches in Crete are newer, the concerns in the Epistle written to Titus focus less upon false teaching and more on the church as God's people in the world.

The dominant theme in this epistle is good works and exemplary Christian behavior for the sake of outsiders. If Titus' teachings are to be effective, they must be supported by the witness of his own life. He himself is to be the demonstration of all that he teaches.[132] Titus now is presented with the tremendous task of not only talking to men about Christ, but modeling the characteristics of Christ as well. The expectation for Titus is for his teachings to

---

[130] Donald Guthrie, *The Pastoral Epistles: An Introduction and Commentary*, 2nd ed., Tyndale New Testament Commentaries (Leicester: Inter-Varsity, 1990), 62.

[131] J. N. D. Kelly, *A Commentary on the Pastoral Epistles: I Timothy, II Timothy, Titus*, Black's New Testament Commentaries (London: A. & C. Black, 1963), 238.

[132] William Barclay, *The Letters to Timothy, Titus, and Philemon*, Rev. ed., The Daily Study Bible Series. -- Rev. Ed. (Philadelphia: Westminster Press, 1975), 252.

be visible, not just verbal.[133] This is also the expectation for the afterpastor who has been called to a congregation that has been hurt by its previous pastor's unethical behavior. If pastoral trust is to be restored, his or her teaching must be visible, not just verbal.

The letter to Titus opens with greetings from the Apostle to his son and co-laborer in ministry. Then Paul lays out his plans for Titus while in Crete. Essentially, Paul tells Titus to organize the Christian communities on the island by setting up responsible ministers/elders and by combating false teaching.[134] The Apostle gives Titus the qualifications, that he is to use for selecting elders. The qualifications for elders listed in Titus closely resemble the ones found in 1 Timothy chapter three. This was not a coincidence of repetition; it was rather the Apostle demonstrating that standards and qualifications for God's leaders do not vary.

The one qualification Paul devotes special attention to is how the elder must be one who has taught his own family in the faith. "The elder/bishop, manager (steward) of God's household, the church community, demonstrates his aptitude for church leadership by his performance at his own household."[135] The Council and Carthage later laid it down: "Bishops, elders and deacons shall not be ordained to office before they have made all in their own household members of the Catholic Church. The basis for this

---

[133] Ibid., 253.

[134] Kelly, *Commentary on Pastoral*, 229.

[135] Benjamin Fiore and Daniel J. Harrington, *The Pastoral Epistles: First Timothy, Second Timothy, Titus*, Sacra Pagina Series (Collegeville, MN: Liturgical Press, 2007), 201.

teaching is to emphasize the point that leadership begins at home."[136]

The next few verses stress the necessity of leaders possessing Christ-like and moral character. These are necessary qualities if an individual is to be respected and suitable for the position of elder/overseer. Due to the false teaching in Crete, elders must also be able to contradict false teachers. The elder's doctrinal function is to be a teacher and apologist of the gospel.[137] Furthermore, it has been said that, "a Christian official must cleave to the true message as it has been taught. In light of this, the minister must have clear convictions and an understanding of the teaching (presumably that which was passed on by oral tradition, although it may possibly refer to some written records,) and he must be prepared to hold firmly to the truth even in the face of opposition. Only so will he be able to perform the double task of exhorting others and correcting those who contradict the truth."[138] This can only be accomplished by using sound doctrine. For this reason, Paul insists that Titus, and those whom he would choose to be elders, be rooted in sound doctrine.

Being able to contradict false teaching was one major function of Titus and those he appointed as elders. However, they also must be able to refute those who oppose sound doctrine. The Greek verb used here for refute is *elegchein,* which suggests an educative

---

[136] Barclay, *The Letters*, 260.
[137] Lea and Griffin, *1,2 Tim, Titus*, 285.
[138] Guthrie, *The Pastoral Epistles*, 198-199.

dimension in confronting false teachers who contradict the gospel message.[139] Another scholar suggests the use of strong medicine for such teachers. "They must be silenced, literally muzzled to prevent their doing their damage."[140]

Having addressed Titus' duties with regard to elders and false teaching, Paul now instructs Titus to teach various groups within the church how to meet certain standards of behavior. Paul singles out five groups to receive specific teaching: older men, older women, young women, young men and slaves. These dynamics make up the demographics of the churches in Crete.[141] Each group is to be taught and challenged to behave in ways consistent with sound doctrine.

The dominant point Paul strives to enforce to Titus is that good behavior flows from sound doctrine, and how divergence from this doctrine can only produce moral disaster and social disorder.[142] By requiring each of the groups to observe a high standard of conduct, Paul is showing concern for the good reputation of the church, as well as for the furtherance of the gospel in an environment of doubtful morality.[143] In the same vein of thought, the Apostle Paul urges Titus to be an example, not simply an exhorter, as stated in the selected passage (Tit 2:7-8). Paul is seeking to accomplish two or three things at once. He is urging younger men to live godly

---

[139] Lea and Griffin, *1,2 Tim, Titus*, 286.
[140] Guthrie, *The Pastoral Epistles,* 199.
[141] Lea and Griffin, *1,2 Tim, Titus*, 295.
[142] Ibid.
[143] Kelly, *Commentary on Pastoral,* 241.

Christian lives, and he is addressing Titus about his particular responsibilities as a minister and as an example to these men.[144]

It is interesting to note, Paul writes more about Titus the example than he does Titus the exhorter. The implication is his teaching will be more effective if it is displayed through his lifestyle rather than just heard via his teachings. The common expression "more is caught than taught" aptly sums up the power of teaching by personal example.[145] Personal example plays a major role in the lives of all clergy. Congregations and communities hear what clergy say through proclamation; however, because of the many unethical acts of some clergy, their voice is sometimes received with uncertainty. Therefore, as Paul emphasizes to Titus, the best way for clergy to teach integrity and moral Christian behavior is to demonstrate it by the way they live.

In chapter 2:7, Titus is given directives as a Christian minister to serve as an example by doing what is good. Simply put, the teachings of Titus will not be effective unless they are supported by his actions in life. Although teaching can refer to what is taught, here it refers primarily to the action of teaching since the qualities that follow apply more naturally to the action than to the content.[146] In matters of content, Titus is instructed to show integrity and seriousness in his teaching. The motive of his

---

[144] George W. Knight, *Commentary on the Pastoral Epistles* (Grand Rapids, MI: Wm. B. Eerdmans Publishing Company, 1992), 311.
[145] Lea and Griffin, *1,2 Tim, Titus*, 304.
[146] Bruce Manning Metzger, David Allan Hubbard, and Glenn W. Barker, *Word Biblical Commentary* (Waco, TX: Word Books, 1982), 413.

teaching must be pure, absent of any desire for personal gain.[147] Barclay echoes this sentiment when he says, "The Christian teacher and preacher is always faced with certain temptations. There is always the danger of self-display, the temptation to demonstrate one's own cleverness and to seek to attract notice to oneself rather than to God's message. There is always temptation to power. The teacher, preacher or pastor is always confronted with temptation to be a dictator. Leader he/she must be, but dictator never. He will find that men can be led, but that they will not be driven. If there is one standard of success which confronts the Christian teacher and preacher more than another, it is to set before himself the wrong standards of success."[148]

This is essential to note as it relates to clergy misconduct since most of the downfalls of clergy are based on selfish desires. Financial impropriety, sexual misconduct, and abuse of power can all be traced back to selfish desires. All of which have caused problems in the lives of clergy and churches throughout history. Therefore, Paul's instructions to Titus, concerning his behavior as a leader are relevant to all clergy.

Moreover, when Paul used the word integrity in v.7 (In everything set them an example by doing what is good. In your teaching show integrity, seriousness), he used a Greek word (*aphthoria*) which denotes untaintedness in teaching as a direct

---

[147] Kelly, *Commentary on Pastoral*, 242.
[148] Barclay, *The Letters*, 253.

contrast to the false teaching in vogue. The same verse also contains the word seriousness (*semnotes*) which emphasizes that if a Christian teacher is to earn respect he must teach in a serious manner.[149] The presentation of the message is to be characterized by dignity and inspire respect in the hearers.[150] According to Moulton and Milligan, it suggests what Latin authors would describe as gravitas, a word that evokes seriousness and formality. Titus's teaching should be respectful in every way.[151] Barclay states, "Dignity is not aloofness, or arrogance, or pride; it is the consciousness of having the terrible responsibility of being the ambassador of Christ. Other men may stoop to pettiness; he must be above it. Other men may bear their grudges; he must have no bitterness. Other men may be touchy about their place; he must have a humility which has forgotten that it has a place. Other men may grow irritable or blaze into anger in an argument; he must have a serenity which cannot be provoked. Nothing so injures the cause of Christ as for the leaders of the Church and the pastors of the people to descend to conduct and to words unbefitting an envoy of Christ."[152]

In v.8, Paul reminds Titus he must have soundness of speech that cannot be condemned. The challenge here is for Titus to propagate the truth of the Gospel and not his own ideas. Once he

---

[149] Guthrie, *The Pastoral Epistles*, 207.
[150] Lea and Griffin, *1,2 Timothy, Titus*, 304.
[151] W. Hulitt Gloer, *1& 2 Timothy-Titus* (Macon, GA: Smyth & Helwys, 2010), 58.
[152] Barclay, *The Letters*, 253.

becomes a propagandist either for his own ideas or for some sectional interest, he ceases to be an effective preacher or teacher of the word of God.[153] The instructions for Titus to be an example of good behavior and teach with integrity, seriousness, and soundness of speech prevented those who opposed him from having anything negative to say.

Hypocrisy in what the minister teaches, or in his or her personal lifestyle, gives those who oppose ammunition for personal attacks. Therefore, integrity is always in order. All adversaries are to be silenced by finding nothing that they can say to their discredit. Philip Schaff and John Chrysostom say, "For when the life is illustrious, and the discourse corresponds to it, being meek and gentle, and affording no handle to the adversaries, it is of unspeakable advantage. Of great use then is the ministry of the word, not any common word, but that which is approved, and cannot be condemned, affording no pretext to those who are willing to censure it."[154]

Therefore, Titus is to remember that he is the official spokesman of the Church, and the world will judge it from what he does and teaches.[155] This does not mean that those who oppose will not attack the Christian church or its message. The idea is that the minister should present no legitimate opportunity for his opponents

[153] Ibid.
[154] John Chrysostom, Philip Schaff, Nicene and Post-Nicene Father First Series Vol. XIII (New York: Christian Literature Company, 1889), 533.
[155] E.F. Scott, *The Moffatt New Testament Commentary: The Pastoral Epistles* (London: Hodder And Stoughton 1947), 165-166.

to use an evil report against them.[156] Furthermore, the goal in this epistle is not for the Cretan society to think well of Christians, but rather for Titus and other church members to behave in such a way that no justifiable charges could be leveled against them.

The overall message is one which summons Titus, and all those who walk in similar shoes, to be examples of Christ-like character in word and deed. The power of one's teaching is best displayed when one's witness is consistent with his or her walk. When what an individual teaches is evident in his or her life, it provides a visible example of Christ-like behavior. Christ-like behavior is what the afterpastor need to exemplify when rebuilding and restoring hope in a hurting congregation.

---

[156] Guthrie, *The Pastoral Epistles,* 208.

Dr. Vernon D. Shelton, Sr.

CHAPTER SIX

A THEOLOGICAL APPROACH TO REBUILDING A WOUNDED CONGREGATION

Practical Theology

Every church will inevitably encounter some type of conflict or challenging situation. Conflict cannot be avoided totally, because the cost of progress may conflict with some individual or organization.[157] Unfortunately, some churches have endured such intense pain and devastation from situations that have occurred from which they never fully recovered. For example, many churches that experienced clergy misconduct recovered physically, yet still struggled mentally, emotionally, and spiritually. The offender has been removed from the church, but the pain and anger still resides within the congregation. When this happens, often times the clergy member that follows encounters suspicion, a lack of trust and unfair treatment, which can result in a premature

---

[157] James H. Harris, *Pastoral Theology: A Black-Church Perspective* (Minneapolis: Fortress Press, 1991), 86.

resignation, creating another set of problems for the congregation.[158]

Although some conflict and problems within the church cannot be avoided, the premature resignation of an afterpastor does not have to be the end result. With the right knowledge and skills, a church who has endured clergy misconduct can be rebuilt, and the afterpastor can have a successful pastorate. Practical theology seeks to give the necessary knowledge and skills to handle conflict in the church from a practical and biblical perspective. With that in mind, this chapter focuses on practical theology.

Over the years, practical theology has undergone numerous definitions. One practical theologian defined it as a theoretical undertaking, which builds on a practical basis.[159] In *Introduction to Theology*, Owen C. Thomas defines practical theology as "the study of practice of the church and its members, including the norms, principles, and visions that guide such practices. This area begins with the doctrine of the church and asks what the church must do in order to be the church–both what is essential and necessary, and what is helpful and edifying. It includes homiletics, liturgics, education, pastoral care, and faith."[160]

[158] Shupe, Stacey, and Darnell, *Bad Pastors,* 220.
[159] Gerben Heitink, *Practical Theology: History, Theory, Action Domains: Manual for Practical Theology*, Studies in Practical Theology (Grand Rapids, MI: W.B. Eerdmans Pub. Co., 1999), 1.
[160] Owen C. Thomas and Ellen K. Wondra, *Introduction to Theology*, 3rd ed. (Harrisburg, PA: Morehouse, 2002), 17.

The Dictionary of Pastoral Care and Counseling defines Practical Theology in a threefold manner.

1) A field of study in clergy education covering the responsibilities and activities of the minister and usually including preaching, liturgics, pastoral care, Christian education, and church polity and administration.

2) An area or discipline in clergy education whose subject matter is the life and activity of the church as it exists in the present.

3) An area or discipline of theology whose subject matter is Christian practice and which brings to bear theological criteria on contemporary situations realms of individual and social action.[161]

The Blackwell Reader in Pastoral and Practical Theology say, "Practical theology is a place where religious belief, tradition and practice meets contemporary experience, questions and conducts a dialogue that is mutually enriching, intellectually critical, and practically transforming."[162] Practical theology, as stated by Dale Andrews "holds in deliberation theological revelation, theoretical science, and the practice of ministry. Therein exists a critical relationship between theology, theory and practice. This

---

[161] James Woodward, Stephen Pattison, and John Patton, *The Blackwell Reader in Pastoral and Practical Theology* (Oxford, UK: Malden, Mass.: Blackwell Publishers, 2000), 5.
[162] Ibid., 7.

relationship should not be understood in any linear notion. Practical theology is not simply a science of diagnosis and application within a selective discipline, like some areas of ministry. Rather, practical theology is an engaging process between theology, theory, and practice with each one feeding upon the others."[163]

Practical theology owes its origin to a modern theologian named Friedrich Schleiermacher. "Schleiermacher was known not only for his contribution to the establishment of theology and practical theology as academic disciplines, but also for his social engagement. His view of the task of practical theology, namely to reflect on the rules of Christian leadership, was not only concerned with practical theology as an academic discipline, it was also concerned with society and societal issues. In short, his theory of Christianity focused not only on the church, but on the church within society."[164] It was Schleiermacher who recognized the value of the Enlightenment, and wanted to build a bridge to modern humanity by reflecting on Christian faith on the basis of the experience of the subject.[165]

---

[163] Dale P. Andrews, Practical Theology for Black Churches: Bridging Black Theology & African American Folk Religion, 1st ed. (Louisville, KY: Westminster John Knox Press, 2002), 1.

[164] Wilhelm Grab, *Secularization Theories, Religious Identity and Practical Theology* (Berlin: Lit Verlag GMBH & CO., 2009), 61.

[165] Heitink, *Practical Theology*, 19.

The term Enlightenment describes what this period did with regard to raising certain issues to the consciousness of the people—a process that has its impact even today. An enlightened person has become a different kind of person. Each has become the subject of his or her own experience. This leads to a new understanding of religion and church that rebels against all forms of authoritarian faith and develops through subjective reflection and rational deliberation.[166]

However, practical theology emerged in the German Protestant tradition as part of the academic theological curriculum in the late eighteenth century. For years, practical theology served as a collective name for a number of dissimilar disciplines with one basic common denominator, which was the ministerial practice.[167] Practical theology has been frequently thought of as applied theology, but the "applied theology" only refers to the task of ministry, not the individual or social aspects of moral life.[168] Applied theology is similar to pastoral care or pastoral theology. Although pastoral care was seen as one of the most important areas of concern in practical theology, its concerns extended beyond this to include other areas of ministry.[169]

---

[166] Ibid.
[167] Ibid., 20.
[168] Don S. Browning, *Practical Theology*, 1st ed. (San Francisco: Harper & Row, 1983), 32.
[169] Woodward, Pattison, and Patton, *The Blackwell Reader*, 2.

Practical theology as stated by Woodward, "concentrates on the actions, issues and events, which are of human significance in the contemporary world. While it is possible to study certain issues such as family, marriage, or poverty in a theoretical way, practical theologians take note with such issues because they wish to have an impact upon them."[170] Ultimately, the work of practical theology is to help generate concepts, norms and actions, which will be of practical utility and make a difference.[171]

Furthermore, theology is practical when it enables the living community to reflect upon and guide its own actions in the context of God's continuing action. Some of the questions that may arise with practical theology are, "What is God doing among us?" or "What is God calling us to become?" These questions require a clear understanding of scripture and hermeneutics.[172] Anderson suggests, "Practical theology needs a solid theological foundation in order that the 'practical' not overwhelm and determine the theological. At the same time, the subject matter of theology is not embedded in the historical consciousness of the community in the form of creeds and dogma alone. Rather theology must continue to reflect on the contemporary work of the Holy Spirit as the praxis of

---

[170] Ibid., 6.
[171] Ibid., 7.
[172] Ibid., 10.

the risen Christ."[173] The task of practical theology as Karl Barth construed it, is to clarify the presuppositions of church praxis.[174]

Additionally, practical theology takes the insights and resources of the Christian religious traditions of belief and practice, such as the Bible, theology and liturgy, as primary resources for its understanding and activity.[175] The aim is to make a contribution to Christian theology and understanding.[176] Any issue of practical human and religious concern may become the focus for practical theological consideration. The subject matters' practical theologians are most concerned with are those that relate to church practice, or those which cause problems in the church. In general, practical theology aspires to be transformative in its theory and practice.

Since practical theology deals with the practices of the church that cause problems and provides a practical model to transform those practices, it is clearly a tool that should be used in a church that has experienced clergy misconduct. When a church has experienced clergy misconduct, not only does the church need to examine the behavior and practices of the minister, they must also review their own systems and practices. This will enable healing to take place and prevent those behaviors from happening again. If a member of the clergy has misused the finances of the church, the

---

[173] Ray Sherman Anderson, *The Shape of Practical Theology: Empowering Ministry with Theological Praxis* (Downers Grove, IL: InterVarsity Press, 2001), 46.
[174] Ibid., 14.
[175] Woodward, Pattison, and Patton, *The Blackwell Reader*, 9.
[176] Ibid.

church should put systems in place that will prevent a reoccurring act, not just discipline the clergy.

One of the major discussions in practical theology is the issue of the relation of theory to practice. As Anderson puts it, "If theory precedes and determines practice, then practice tends to be primarily concerned with methods, techniques and strategies for ministry, lacking theological substance. If practice takes priority over theory, ministry tends to be based on pragmatic results rather than prophetic revelation. A praxis approach does not ignore theory, but develops theory in an interactional model with praxis. All good practice includes theory."[177] Ammerman states that, "Practical theology moves from life to faith and then back to life (practice to theory to practice)."[178]

The great theologian Karl Barth resisted all attempts to portray theory and praxis in opposition to one another.[179] In his early work, *Church Dogmatics,* Barth describes "the distinction between theoretical and practical as a primal lie, which has to be resisted in principal. The understanding of Christ as the light of life can be understood only as a theory which has its origin and goal in praxis."[180] To fully understand the concept that Barth is making, it

---

[177] Ray Sherman Anderson, *Spiritual Caregiving as Secular Sacrament : A Practical Theology for Professional Caregivers*, Practical Theology Series (London ; New York: J. Kingsley Publishers, 2003), 17.
[178] Nancy Tatom Ammerman, *Studying Congregations: A New Handbook* (Nashville, TN: Abingdon Press, 1998), 25.
[179] Ibid.
[180] Anderson, *Spiritual Caregiving,* 17-18.

is critical that practice not be confused with praxis. Praxis is quite different from the mere application of truth or theory; praxis links truth to action. In *The Soul of Ministry: Forming Leaders for God's People,* Anderson informs, "The one who utilizes praxis must have discernment of the ultimate goal that is becoming evident through the action. It is also the case, that only in the process of the action itself that certain truths concerning the final purpose or goal are discovered. This is what makes praxis quite different from practice as application through technique or skill."[181]

To further illustrate this point, Anderson used the example of John the Baptist and the act of baptism:

> John was practicing baptism with the purpose of producing repentance. When Jesus came to be baptized by John, he was reluctant because he recognized Jesus as being the 'Lamb of God who takes away the sins of the world.' John realized the future had entered into the present, and what began as a practice, became praxis. Through the practice of baptism, John discovered the praxis of the Spirit. John pointed to the future, which had become visible in the present. He did not predict the future as the prophets had done, he pointed to it and announced its presence. He exercised his gift of discernment.[182]

Therefore, the term praxis refers to the unity of purposeful activity and the thoughtful consideration of that activity. Praxis as stated by Poling, "always involves engagement of the self, the

---

[181] Ray Sherman Anderson, *The Soul of Ministry: Forming Leaders for God's People,* 1st ed. (Louisville, KY: Westminster John Knox Press, 1997), 27.
[182] Ibid., 28.

network of decisions leading from the past into the present and the future."[183]

Practical Theology as a Crisis Discipline

From a historical perspective, practical theology can be viewed as a crisis discipline. During the nineteenth century, the western society experienced a major crisis of authority. The authority of parents, teachers, politicians, and spiritual leaders was no longer accepted at face value. The process of democratization changed the way decisions were made, eliminating the power resting with one individual or group. It became a shared responsibility.[184] At the same time, many churches were going through a similar crisis concerning the authority of Scripture, the authority of clergy, and spiritual authority in the church. This came about mostly as a result of multiple cases of clergy misconduct in the church, and the lack of punishment that followed.[185]

This new "emancipation" had a major effect on the life of the church as attendance dropped and some parishioners stopped coming to church altogether. "In 1947, 17.1 percent of the Dutch population did not belong to any church. In 1979, 52 percent of all Dutch men and women no longer considered themselves members of any church. For the first time, the church in the Netherlands

---

[183] James N. Poling and Donald E. Miller, *Foundations for a Practical Theology of Ministry* (Nashville, TN: Abingdon Press, 1985), 64.
[184] Heitink, *Practical Theology*, 2.
[185] Ibid., 3

found itself in the minority position. In 1964, the first chair for practical theology was initiated at the Catholic University in Nijmegen."[186]

The theological department of this university was founded in 1923; yet, up to this point, they felt no need for a discipline or department in practical theology. Mainly this was so because the clergy were not aware of any particular problems and the Catholic Church believed in their leadership.[187] In 1968, Jacob Firet, the first professor of practical theology of the Free University of Amsterdam, proclaimed the church could no longer continue in its former ways for it no longer had a clear model to follow. With that in mind, he instituted a "theory of action."[188] This "theory of action," which is also considered a theory of crisis, has maintained great significance both then and now.

For example, when a crisis occurs in the church and the traditional approaches of addressing them lose their plausibility, theory of crisis/practical theology provides spiritual and practical ways to respond. For decades, practical theology laid the blueprint for leaders of the church by giving them practical ways to respond to some of the major issues they were facing. A number of clergy who went to pastor a church, that had experienced clergy misconduct ended up resigning early, or found themselves stressed, because they did not have practical ways to respond to all the

---

[186] Ibid., 4
[187] Ibid.
[188] Ibid.

challenges they were facing.[189] When a previous pastor commits financial improprieties, the afterpastor will face skepticism and reservations when dealing with money. One practical way to handle this is for the afterpastor to provide oversight of the financial matters of the church, but not touch money directly.

The majority of leaders and churches will inevitably face some sort of issue, challenge, or conflict within the church. The response or actions taken can either help or hurt the church and its leader. Therefore, it is essential to have a practical approach to deal with conflict in the church. In *Practical Theology: An Introduction*, Richard Osmer developed a framework for leaders and churches to guide their interpretation and response to issues that may arise in the church. This can be helpful in cases where misconduct has taken place.

In this book, Osmer asks four questions to first explore: What is going on in this context? Why is this going on? What ought to be going on? How might the leader respond? To properly answer these questions, he outlines four core tasks to follow:

- The descriptive-empirical task. (Gathering information that helps us discern patterns and dynamics in particular episodes, situations, or context).

---

[189] Friberg and others, *Restoring the Soul of a Church: Healing Congregations Wounded by Clergy Sexual Misconduct,* 60.

- The interpretive task. (Drawing on theories of the arts and sciences to better understand and explain why these patterns and dynamics are occurring).

- The normative task. (Using theological concepts to interpret particular episodes, situations, or context, constructing ethical norms to guide our responses, and learning from good practice).

- The pragmatic task. (Determining strategies of action that will influence situations in ways that are desirable and entering into a reflective conversation).[190]

Together these four tasks constitute the basic structure of practical theological interpretation. It is helpful to conceptualize these four tasks with the image of a hermeneutical circle, which portrays interpretation as composed of distinct but interrelated moments. The four tasks of practical theology interpretation interpenetrate. Problems emerging in a pragmatic task may open up issues that need to be explored empirically. Theories used to interpret particular events may bring to the forefront issues calling for normative reflection. The interaction and mutual influence of all four tasks distinguish practical theology from other fields.[191]

---

[190] Richard Robert Osmer, *Practical Theology: An Introduction* (Grand Rapids, MI: William B. Eerdmans Pub. Co., 2008), 4.

[191] Ibid., 10.

Practical Theology and Church Conflict

One area practical theology has potential to be the most effective is conflict in the church. Conflict is part of the human predicament and it is seemingly endless. All pastors and congregations will undoubtedly encounter some form of conflict while engaged in ministry. A study conducted at Hartford Institute for Religious Research concluded, "Here in the United States, conflict is a synonym for congregation. The same study stated that 75 percent of congregations reported some level of conflict in the past five years. Yet, another study cites conflict and the stress it causes as the leading cause for pastors involuntarily leaving the church."[192]

Practical theology plays a major role in terms of church conflict. It offers biblical insight and tools that can assist pastors and congregations in the resolution process. Churches can face numerous types of obstacles and conflict. For example, churches may clash over financial struggles, values, division, liturgy, loss of membership, theology, and ethical issues concerning the pastor. All of which can cause major setbacks for any congregation. Conflict within the church can leave believers confused and torn inwardly, ultimately pushing them away from the church. When a church is divided, it creates tension and a lack of trust among the congregation. Dissension of this nature typically tends to be

---

[192] Alfred Poirier, *The Peacemaking Pastor: A Biblical Guide to Resolving Church Conflict* (Grand Rapids, MI: Baker Books, 2006), 9.

stressful for the leadership as well as the membership. However, if the congregation is divided due to clergy misconduct, it creates a whole new set of problems.

When churches experience conflict because of clergy misconduct, in addition to experiencing hurt and betrayal, they become socially and spiritually divided.[193] "In one congregation, where the pastor had been voted out, a division was apparent when those who were loyal to him objected to a new pastoral candidate. After much discussion and tears, members came to a consensus, but the disunity from the previous pastoral conflict was evident."[194] In some cases, members' love and commitment to the pastor will cause them to look beyond their issues and foster restoration. In other cases, congregations remove the pastor from the church, and take their pain and frustration out on the individual who follows. For many congregations, after they have experienced clergy misconduct, they lose trust in the office of the minister.

In the book, *Restoring the Soul of the Church*, Hopkins state that when misconduct happens, defenses rise up and multiple questions arise such as, "How can I trust clergy again?"[195] It is also important to remember that when a congregation removes a pastor it does not guarantee the removal of all of their issues. Ousting the pastor may bring some relief from tension, but if only one aspect of the situation is addressed the congregation may find themselves

[193] Dave Peters, *Surviving Church Conflict* (Scottdale, PA: Herald Press, 1997), 16.
[194] Ibid, 17.
[195] Gaede and Benyei, *When a Congregation*, 56.

in danger of repeating the cycle. If the latter does take place, it will manufacture even greater hurt on the congregation when they begin wondering what is wrong with them.

Moreover, in conflict resolution, it is vital to remember the conflict is not against individuals, but it is a spiritual battle between the holy and the unholy. The church is called to conform to the holy. In addition, Christians should always be mindful that God is in the midst of every human battle to resolve conflict. "In the church, our generation may be too quick to endorse checklist strategies to resolve our conflicts and build our churches. We need to emphasize the spiritual method taught in the Scriptures. The spiritual formula for conflict resolution is the implementation of God's grace in the lives of each member of a congregation."[196]

Although conflict within the church often promotes division, lack of trust and broken relationships, these relationships can be reconciled and restored. In the book, *Congregations Alive*, Donald Smith declares, "A congregation can become a loving, caring community only if there are face-to-face relationships between individuals as authentic persons. Close relationships, in turn, are possible only in a climate of trust and mutual support. Mutual trust is an essential ingredient if people are ever going to share their vulnerabilities with each other."[197] Furthermore, renewal comes when a climate of acceptance and trust gives freedom to be honest

---

[196] Peters, *Surviving Church Conflict*, 27.
[197] Donald P. Smith, *Congregations Alive*, 1st ed. (Philadelphia: Westminster Press, 1981), 83.

with one another about fears and failures, about vulnerabilities and longings. It also comes when receptive reconciliation can be experienced within the Christian context of community.[198]

---

[198] Ibid., 108.

CHAPTER SEVEN

FROM THEORY TO PRACTICE

One of the major barriers or challenges in rebuilding and restoring hope in a congregation that experienced clergy misconduct, is many congregants internalize their pain and rarely share it with the afterpastor. This happens due to many congregants losing trust and confidence in pastors after experiencing clergy misconduct. Sadly, instead of discussing their pain and disappointment with the afterpastor, many congregants mishandle their pain. They treat the afterpastor as if he or she was the perpetrator. A church with these types of challenges and behaviors is not easy to pastor. A great deal of love, compassion, patience, integrity, and teaching is needed to begin the rebuilding and healing process. In addition, the afterpastor must strategically cultivate an environment where love, healing, and restoration can take place. This is not an easy thing to accomplish when members are not open and fully honest with the afterpastor about all that took place prior to his or her arrival. However, it is necessary if the afterpastor is going to be successful in moving the church forward.

One way to begin the healing process with a hurting congregation is through a focus group. Focus groups are cost effective and a great way to collect information from several people quickly. In addition, focus groups are good for getting rich data in participants' own words and developing deeper insight as to how they really feel. They are mainly used to gauge people's reactions and feelings to items or incidents. When a congregation has been hurt, this is a great way to discuss what took place and assist them with moving forward.

The Focus Group

Due to the sensitive nature of the issues and emotions involved with this type of research, I determined the best method to use was mixed methods. According to Creswell, "There is more insight to be gained from the combination of both qualitative and quantitative research than either form by itself. Their combined use provides an expanded understanding of research problems."[199] The sequential exploratory strategy was used for data collection and interpretation. This type of strategy "involves a first phase of qualitative data collection and analysis, followed by a second phase of quantitative data collection that builds on the results of the first qualitative phase. Weight is generally placed on the first phase, and the data is connected between the qualitative data

---

[199] John W. Creswell, *Research Design: Qualitative, Quantitative, and Mixed Methods Approaches*, 3rd ed. (Thousand Oaks, CA: Sage Publications, 2009), 203.

analysis and the quantitative data collection. The purpose of this strategy is to use quantitative data and results to assist in the interpretation of qualitative findings."[200]

The overall goal was to engage a focus group to obtain honest feedback regarding how they felt about pastors/clergy and the future of the church after experiencing clergy misconduct. Additionally, I desired to see if something could be done to bring about an attitudinal change within the congregation. Based on the writings in the book entitled, *Focus Groups,* I envisioned a focus group as a very effective research method because it "encourages participants to share perceptions and points of view, without pressuring participants to vote or reach a consensus."[201] Therefore, I felt a focus group would provide "a way to better understand how people feel about an issue."[202] For those who wish to do a focus group in their church, it can be done in the form of bible studies, workshops or small groups. All three methods, if done with an evaluation, will provide some measurable data.

The methods I chose to use when gathering measurable data for this book was workshops and Bible Studies. I opted to use these two methods because I believed them to be the best opportunity to have constructive dialogue with members of the congregation. It is in these settings, congregants can express what they feel, ask

---

[200] Ibid., 211.

[201] Richard A. Krueger and Mary Anne Casey, *Focus Groups: A Practical Guide for Applied Research*, 3rd ed. (Thousand Oaks, CA: Sage Publications, 2000), 4.

[202] Ibid., 4.

questions, and engage the pastor/presenter in conversation. In addition, it gives the pastor/presenter settings in which he or she can lead discussions and ask questions of congregants without them feeling pressured to answer. Although there are other opportunities for the pastors to communicate with the congregants, I felt workshops and Bible Studies were the more intimate and safest forum to engage them.

Moreover, to get the best data for this type of project, the focus group should consist of congregants who were active during the previous administration, and stayed at the church during the time of transition. The size of the group may vary; however, I recommend no less than twenty. This will ensure that there is enough measurable data. The group should represent the demographics of the church, with each gender and age group represented. The group should also contain a mixture of leaders and laypeople.

I recommend a total of six workshops, bible studies, or small group sessions. The standard for whatever method used should be that they are biblically based, address the personal, emotional, and spiritual issues of the congregation, and include helpful suggestions for practical application. The attitudes of the group should be tested twice using a pre and post-survey, once prior to the workshops and again at the completion of the workshops. This will help the facilitator understand the attitudes of the group before and after the workshops are completed. Also, it will give the facilitator measurable data as it relates to the effectiveness of the content that was taught. Copies of a sample pre and post survey can be found in Appendix A.

In addition to the pre and post-survey, I recommend that an evaluation be given at the end of each workshop to measure the effectiveness of the subject matter, the impact it had on their life, and if it prompted a behavioral or an attitudinal change. A sample copy of a workshop evaluation form can be found in Appendix B. After the workshops are completed, and the post-survey has been administered, analysis can be made to see if an attitudinal change has occurred or if more work has to be done.

Finally, while conducting the focus group I recommend that the afterpastor use this time to engage the members in a personal, yet professional way in order to build a better relationship with the group. If the afterpastor and members of the group can develop a closer relationship, the group would be more willing to open up about what they have experienced. This concept was extracted from the book, *Ministerial Ethics: Moral Formation for Church Leaders*, written by Joe E. Trull and James E. Carter. In the book, Trull and Carter suggests:

> Relationships between a minister and the members of a congregation are essential. Does a minister view the congregation as a friend or foe? Do the members look upon the minister as a friend who will care for them, or as a foe whom they ought to resist and whose teachings, motives, and methods they ought to question? The way a minister and members view one another depends on the relationships they have with one another. To a large degree, those relationships depend on the ministry skills the

minister displays with them. Relationships are more important in ministry than in any other profession.

Many issues in churches are decided based on whether members love and trust their ministers, not on the issues themselves. Good relationships between ministers and congregations must be developed. How are they developed? They are developed in the normal course of ministry. As pastors bury the dead, visit the sick, comfort families, marry people, and generally share in living with people, they build lasting relationships. Through compassionate care and genuine concern, a minister lets people know that they are meaningful and important. And all of this rest on the personal integrity of the minister.[203]

The Workshops/Bible Studies

During the workshops/Bible Studies, conversations are to be encouraged and participants should be given freedom to discuss the topic presented, or anything else that may come to their mind during the presentation. Below is an overview of the six workshops I used during the focus group sessions I conducted as a part of my research.

1. *Session One: The Nature and Effects of Clergy Misconduct* – This workshop provided the participants a clear understanding of clergy misconduct on all levels. It also gave biblical examples of clergy misconduct as well as the effects clergy misconduct has on its victims, the congregation, and the afterpastor.

---

[203] Joe E. Trull and James E. Carter, *Ministerial Ethics: Moral Formation for Church Leaders*, 2nd ed. (Grand Rapids, MI: Baker Academic, 2004), 89-90.

2. *Session Two: How Should We Respond* – This workshop provided practical ways in which the congregation should respond spiritually and legally to accusations and incidents of clergy misconduct. This included the church's responsibility to the pastor and his family, the victim and his/her family. This workshop also discussed the need for pastoral care for congregations in crisis.

3. Session Three: *The Power to Forgive* – This workshop provided biblical principals about forgiveness. It also challenged the participants to do what God requires by forgiving those who have hurt or disappointed them as it relates to clergy misconduct.

4. Session Four: *From Hurt to Healing* –This workshop challenged the participants to face their issues or pain produced by clergy misconduct and work toward their healing.

5. Session Five: *Proper Boundaries and Safe Relationships* – This workshop provided tools for building proper pastoral and congregant relationships within the church. This session also discussed fair and unfair treatment of the afterpastor/successor.

6. Session Six: *Putting the Pieces Back Together* – This workshop highlighted biblical examples from Nehemiah chapter 2:17-28 and Titus 2:6-7 detailing what should take place in order for the congregation and afterpastor to begin the rebuilding process.

The Results of the Workshops

A survey was given to each member of the group prior to the sessions and at the conclusion of the sessions to determine if there was an attitudinal change.

The Pre & Post Survey Results

Members of the focus group were asked to circle the number/statement that best represents their viewpoint or knowledge.

1 Strongly Disagree   2 Disagree   3 Agree   4 Strongly Agree

Statement 1 - I have a lot of knowledge about clergy misconduct.

	Pre-Survey	Post-Survey
1 Strongly Disagree	45%	0%
2 Disagree	40%	0%
3 Agree	10%	45%
4 Strongly Agree	5%	55%

Analysis of Data

At the beginning of the workshops, 85 percent of the group either disagreed or strongly disagreed to having a lot of knowledge about clergy misconduct. After completing the workshop entitled, "The Nature and Effects of Clergy Misconduct," 100 percent of the group either agreed or strongly agreed to have a wealth of knowledge about clergy misconduct. The results of the pre and post survey revealed an 85 percent increase in the knowledge of the focus group pertaining to clergy misconduct. The cause for the shift in knowledge is attributed to the workshop clearly defining clergy misconduct on all levels, as well as how it affects the victims, the perpetrator's family, the church, and the community. The workshop also addressed how clergy misconduct affects the afterpastor/successor.

Statement 2 - I have a lot of knowledge about how the church (should) handle clergy misconduct spiritually and legally.

	Pre-Survey	Post-Survey
1 Strongly Disagree	65%	0%
2 Disagree	25%	0%
3 Agree	10%	35%
4 Strongly Agree	0%	65%

Analysis of Data

Initially, 90 percent of the participants either disagreed or strongly disagreed that they were knowledgeable about how a church should handle clergy misconduct spiritually and legally. The results from the post-survey reflected a 90 percent change in knowledge. The change was a direct result of completing the workshop, "How Should We Respond." After attending the workshop, the participants demonstrated they are significantly more knowledgeable about how the church should respond spiritually and legally to cases of clergy misconduct. For instance, prior to the workshop, several group members believed the only valid response was to get rid of the pastor. However, by attending the sessions, they learned the process of investigating the matter, the need to meet with all parties involved, the necessity of legal advice and spiritual guidance, and lastly, the church's responsibility to the victim, the victim's family, and the family of the clergy member.

Statement 3 - I am still angry or disappointed with the previous pastor:

	Pre-Survey	Post-Survey
1 Strongly Disagree	0%	30%
2 Disagree	5%	50%
3 Agree	35%	15%
4 Strongly Agree	60%	5%

Analysis of Data

When the project first began, 95 percent of the group either agreed or strongly agreed they were still angry or disappointed with the previous pastor. After completing six sessions of the project model, the post survey revealed a 75 percent attitudinal change occurred within a number of the participants. Prior to the workshops, a mere 5 percent disagreed they were still angry or disappointed with the previous pastor. However after the workshops, 80 percent of the group either disagreed or strongly disagreed to possessing anger or disappointment with the previous pastor.

Statement 4 - Clergy who have been found guilty of clergy misconduct can be trusted again.

	Pre-Survey	Post-Survey
1 Strongly Disagree	75%	60%
2 Disagree	25%	15%
3 Agree	0%	25%
4 Strongly Agree	0%	0%

Analysis of Data

Initially, 100 percent of the group either disagreed or strongly disagreed with the belief that clergy who commits clergy misconduct can be trusted again. After completing the workshops, the post survey revealed there was not a significant change in the group's attitude. The post survey results showed only 25 percent of the group had changed their opinion regarding clergy being trusted again after they have been found guilty of misconduct. In this case, it appears most group participants held true to the old mantra: once lost, trust is a hard thing to regain.

Statement 5 – After experiencing clergy misconduct, I do not trust or have confidence in any pastor/clergyperson.

	Pre-Survey	Post-Survey
1 Strongly Disagree	5%	10%
2 Disagree	10%	45%
3 Agree	35%	40%
4 Strongly Agree	50%	5%

Analysis of Data

At the beginning of the project, 85 percent of the group either agreed or strongly agreed to no longer trusting or having confidence in pastors/clergy as result of what they have experienced. After attending the workshops, the post survey revealed that there was significant change in attitude among the group members. The results from the post survey showed a 40 percent change, for this time, only 45 percent of the group agreed or strongly agreed that they do not trust or have lost confidence in pastors/clergy. Some of the participants pointed out that building trust and confidence takes time, and as they get to know the individual their feelings may change. Other members of the group reminded them all pastors and clergy persons are not the same, and therefore, everyone deserves a fair chance.

Statement 6 - I am likely to give clergy a second chance after they have been found guilty of misconduct.

	Pre-Survey	Post-Survey
1 Strongly Disagree	70%	15%
2 Disagree	25%	25%
3 Agree	5%	50%
4 Strongly Agree	0%	10%

Analysis of Data

At the beginning of the project, 95 percent of the group either disagreed or strongly disagreed to the likelihood of giving clergy another chance if they were found guilty of misconduct. After completing the workshops, a significant change took place.

The results from the post survey revealed a 55 percent change in attitude towards clergy who have been found guilty of misconduct. Prior to the workshops, only 5 percent of the group was inclined to give a clergy person a second chance. However, after the workshops, this number increased to 60 percent of the group agreed or strongly agreed to granting clergy another chance. The cause for the shift was heavily attributed to the workshops entitled, "The Power to Forgive," and "From Hurt to Healing," both of which dealt with forgiveness and second chances. These workshops enabled the participants to recognize no one is perfect, and God has given everyone a second chance. The group also learned that God can use people even after they have made mistakes.

Statement 7- Clergy misconduct has lessened my faith in God.

	Pre-Survey	Post-Survey
1 Strongly Disagree	60%	60%
2 Disagree	35%	35%
3 Agree	5%	5%
4 Strongly Disagree	0%	0%

Analysis of Data

The data gleaned from this survey revealed there was no change of attitude in this area. Originally, 95 percent of the group believed their experiences of clergy misconduct did not lesson or affect their faith in God. The post-survey revealed 95 percent felt the same way.

Statement 8 - I am afraid that clergy misconduct will be repeated in my church.

	Pre-Survey	Post-Survey
1 Strongly Disagree	0%	10%
2 Disagree	5%	55%
3 Agree	40%	20%
4 Strongly Agree	55%	15%

Analysis of Data

When the project first started, 95 percent of the participants agreed or strongly agreed they were fearful clergy misconduct would be repeated in the church. However, upon completion of the various sessions, a significant change took place. The post survey demonstrated 60 percent of the group had changed the way they felt concerning the future of the church and the integrity of the pastor. Prior to the focus group's discussions only 5 percent disagreed to being afraid the church could potentially experience clergy misconduct again. After spending time in the sessions, more than half, 65 percent to be precise, of the group disagreed or strongly disagreed they were fearful that clergy misconduct would be repeated. Throughout the six-week time period, the writer intentionally spent time building a rapport with the participants and establishing relationships, largely because time and interacting with the pastor helps congregants build confidence in the clergy's abilities and intentions.

Statement 9 - Even years later, I am still ashamed of the clergy misconduct that took place in my church.

	Pre-Survey	Post-Survey
1 Strongly Disagree	0%	10%
2 Disagree	25%	25%
3 Agree	35%	30%
4 Strongly Agree	40%	35%

Analysis of Data

Not a great deal of change occurred in this area. Initially, 75 percent of the group either agreed or strongly agreed that even several years later, they were still ashamed of what took place in the church. Although some members have begun to openly discuss what transpired, the post survey revealed they still possess some embarrassment. The results from the post survey showed 65percent

agreed or strongly agreed they are still ashamed years after the incident took place.

Statement 10 – I am pleased with the direction the church is moving under the current pastor.

	Pre-Survey	Post Survey
1 Strongly Disagree	0%	0%
2 Disagree	15%	5%
3 Agree	65%	45%
4 Strongly Agree	20%	55%

Analysis of Data

There was slight movement with this question. In the beginning, 85 percent of the group either agreed or strongly agreed they were pleased with the direction of the church under the current pastor. After the project model was completed, this number rose to 90 percent either agreed or strongly agreed they were satisfied with the direction of the church under its current pastor. This statistic represents signs of hope among the membership regarding the future of their church.

Conclusion

At the conclusion of the focus group sessions, the members expressed interest in conducting some type of follow-up in order to bring a sense of closure to a dark past. It was also suggested these workshops be offered church-wide or taught in a bible study setting due to the impact they had on the group. The focus group began as simply a requirement for the Doctor of Ministry Project; however, it turned out to be just what the church needed to begin rebuilding and healing. The results from the pre and post survey clearly showed an attitudinal change in the members of the group. They also showed that there is hope for rebuilding a church which has been hurt by clergy misconduct.

CHAPTER EIGHT

CONCLUSIONS AND RECOMMENDATIONS

Conclusions

The research revealed that when a church has been hurt by clergy misconduct, it leaves the congregation broken, wounded, and divided. Clergy misconduct affects the church numerically, emotionally, financially and spiritually. When misconduct has occurred some members are left devastated and confused as to how they should move forward, while others may lose confidence not only in the pastor, but in all ministers. Many victims feel they could never trust clergy again, making it hard on the clergyperson whom follows. This makes rebuilding an enormous challenge for the afterpastor. When this happens, often times the afterpastor gets overwhelmed and ends up resigning or suddenly leaving the church, leaving the church in a deeper hole than before.

However, not all situations of clergy misconduct and the afterpastor have to end in a negative way. It is possible for the afterpastor to rebuild the church and have a successful pastorate.

My research has proven that when an afterpastor loves the people, performs the basic pastoral duties well, lives with integrity, develops appropriate relationships with congregants, and teaches sound biblical principles, it will begin the process of restoring trust in the office of minister, restore hope, and foster healing to a hurting congregation. This book also corroborates the belief that attitudes can change when people are taught the biblical way to handle their pain and disappointments. Attitudes can also change when people are given an opportunity to have constructive dialogue about their feelings, fears and reservations, and these same emotions are heard without judgment. In addition, when members gain confidence in the integrity of the afterpastor, as well as hope for the future of the church, attitudes can change. It is my belief that when attitudes change, people change; when people change the church changes. The job of the afterpastor is to change the perception and attitudes of the people and the people will change the attitude and perception of the church.

Things to Remember

In this section I would like to give some practical lessons and things to remember for the afterpastor and church. These are lessons that I have learned from research and personal experiences. It is my intent that these lessons will inform and insist you in the rebuilding process.

For the Afterpastor

Remember:

1) ~ Some Members Will Love Their Pastor No Matter What. Prior to researching this topic, I assumed that when clergy misconduct takes place in a church all of the anger, blame and disappointment were directed towards the pastor. Surprisingly however, I discovered this was not necessarily the case. Not everyone placed all the blame on the previous pastor, in some instances individuals point the finger at the victim. Some people believe the victims does things to bring this on themselves. When this happens it should not divide the church, it opens a door for the afterpastor to teach about proper boundaries and clergy and member relationships.

In addition, when clergy misconduct takes place, some of the pain and anger can stem from how the pastor is treated after the accusations have been disclosed. For example, some of the anger and resentment can be directed towards the church leaders due to the way the situation was handled publicly, legally, and morally. Regardless of the situation, some members will still love their pastor and are of the mindset that the church should never treat anyone badly, especially the pastor, even if they have been found guilty of misconduct.

2) ~ Churches Become Divided When Clergy Misconduct Has Occurred. When clergy misconduct takes place within a church too often it leaves the church divided over who is at fault, and what should be done with the pastor/minister. I want to discuss three groups that will appear in a church that experienced clergy misconduct.

The first group is the *members who are on the pastor's side* and cannot believe the accusations are true. When accusations come out against the pastor, often times they will immediately take the pastor's side. However, even if the accusations are true, these individuals feel that the pastor can or should be restored after a period of discipline. Other than stealing and sexual assault, this group will support their pastor no matter what. One of the worst things an afterpastor can do is come in to the church bashing the previous pastor about what took place. He/she will either lose those members or will have a hard time building a good relationship with them. Therefore, never side with those who negatively talk about the previous pastor; this can become a stumbling block for the afterpastor.

The second group is the *Clergy Killers*. This group feels that regardless how major or minor the issue might be, the pastor should be removed from office immediately. This group does not care about evidence; they just want the pastor gone. In their opinion, anything the pastor does wrong is grounds for dismissal. Majority of the times this group does not like the pastor and they were just waiting for an opportunity to get rid of him/her. This group will do whatever it takes to get rid of the pastor even if they way it is done hurts the church's membership, finances, integrity or reputation.

Afterpastors should be aware of the *Clergy Killers*. The afterpastor will not have to pull information out of this group because they will voluntarily tell him/her how bad the previous pastor was. To them the previous pastor did not do anything right, and they will justify their own actions even if they were unethical. Just remember, what they did to the previous pastor they will also do to the afterpastor. Afterpastors, be aware of *Clergy Killers! And Remember Every Church Has Some!*

The third group is the, *I do not know what to do group*. These are the individuals who are confused, shocked, hurt, devastated and do not know what to do. They support their pastor; however, they stand on what is right and wrong. This group would like to wait until all the information has been given. They also do not think a quick decision should be made without seeking outside counsel. This group will have heated debates with the *Clergy Killers*. Depending on the issue, they may come to the conclusion that the pastor should be dismissed, but they want things to be handled with dignity and integrity. What is clear is that clergy misconduct affects people in different ways, and not everyone responds the same way. Therefore, the afterpastor should never presume to know people's feelings when it comes to clergy misconduct. Take time to get to know the congregation.

3) ~ Time Does Not Heal All Wounds. Contrary to popular opinion, time does not heal all wounds or pain. Neither does calling a new pastor remove the pain, nor negate what took place. Healing and restoration will not take place until the issues of the past and present are properly uncovered and dealt with. The afterpastor will have to first learn what actually took place with the previous pastor, who was affected and how, and then begin planning ways to restore trust and foster healing to a wounded congregation. Restoring trust is a very important step in the rebuilding process because members may not be open with the afterpastor until there is a certain level of trust and confidence. Healing and restoring hope should be a priority of the afterpastor.

4) ~ Do Not Take Everything Personal. When a new pastor is called to a church that experienced some form of clergy misconduct, a lack of trust is to be expected. It is the same in relationships; when you have been hurt in a previous relationship, the next person does not immediately have your trust, they have to earn it. Trust is not given, its earned.

During this process of conducting a focus group, I learned that when there is a lack of trust, or skepticism from members it is not always a personal attack against the afterpastor, for in some cases, it is a defense mechanism. During a conversation with a member she stated, *"She decided not to put her trust in another pastor, because she did not want to get hurt again.*" This statement enabled me to see that all unfair treatment of the afterpastor is not necessarily done with malice. With that said, an afterpastor should not take everything personally, but instead spend time becoming acquainted with the individual. This can possibly set a foundation for a positive, Christ-like relationship. It can also help the person understand that not all clergy are the same.

5) ~ *Love And Care For The People.* When a congregation has been hurt or misused by a pastor, they need to know that the afterpastor really cares about them. When a congregation feels that the afterpastor is not genuine, they will fight everything he/she does to protect their church. On the other hand, when a congregation feels that the afterpastor is genuine and really loves the church, they will be open and more willing to work with the pastor as he/she leads them in a new direction. This is because there is a lack of fear of being taken advantage of. The afterpastor must remember that a hurting congregation is a sensitive congregation that needs a lot of nurturing and love.

For The Church

Remember:

1) ~ *Be Honest About What Happened In the Beginning.* Do not be mistaken, everything will eventually come to the forefront. Therefore, it is important for the church/pulpit committee to be

open and honest in the beginning. Although you may be ashamed of what happened, be honest with each candidate, especially if there is a great deal of interest in the candidate. The worst thing that could happen is for the afterpastor to find out what happened at the church later. It will appear that the committee was not honest with him/her. This hinders the trust relationship that is needed to have a successful team between pastor and people. The afterpastor should know what he/she is facing before they are fully committed to the ministry. It's only fair! Knowing upfront can help the afterpastor in their approach to ministry. Not knowing could set them up for failure, and early departure. Do yourself a favor, be honest upfront!

2) ~ *Remember, All Pastors Are Not The Same.* It is unfair and unethical for the church to   treat the afterpastor as if they committed the misconduct. Many churches show resentment, skepticism, and distrust to the afterpastor because of what they experienced with the previous pastor. Many believers lose trust and confidence in all clergy because of the actions of one. Remember, all ministers are not the same. There are some ministers who lack integrity, however, there are many who walk in integrity and take the call of God on their life seriously. Therefore, the church should never treat a new pastor/afterpastor in a negative way because of one bad experience with another pastor. Everyone deserves a fair chance.

3) ~ Do Not Forget To Minister To The Victim (s). Many times so much happens with the dismissal or disciplining of the pastor that the church forgets to minister to the victims. Professional counseling may be needed, depending on the nature of the situation that took place. If professional counseling is needed, the church should cover the expense. In addition, the church should minister to and assist the pastor's family, as they are also victims. The spouse and children may need counseling or help dealing with what has taken place. Many times the church neglects the pastor's family because of the actions of the pastor. However, the right thing to do is to help them get through this trying time in their lives. Clergy misconduct not only affects the church, it also affects the first family. When clergy misconduct occurs in the church, remember to minister to the victims.

4) When Misconduct Occurs, Always Seek Legal Guidance Before Taking Action. This can keep the church from being sued. Many times churches take actions of discipline based on their spiritual convictions. However, although the church is a place for spiritual worship, it is also a business. This means the business side of things must be handled legally and justly. Just because a pastor or employee does something that's unethical spiritually does not mean the church can just eliminate them. Everything must be done decently and in order, according to the By-Laws and Constitution of the church. Documentation is important! Minutes must be kept for all meetings and legal help is always advised. (Side Note:

Clergy Killers may not be the best people to handle this type of incident in the church. The church may end up in some legal trouble, because Clergy Killers do not care about rules or laws. They just want the pastor gone!)

Recommendations for Further Study

The focus group has proven to be an effective tool to engage the congregation in constructive dialogue and obtain honest feedback about sensitive topics. An aspect that would have made this project even more effective is an increase in the number of youth participants. When I did the focus group, it consisted primarily of adults, with only 5% of the group being between the ages of 12-19. With that in mind, feedback from the youth would have enhanced the data. Youth participation is important because for some youth the pastor is seen as a mentor, father/mother figure, and role model. When misconduct from the pastor occurs, it is not only interesting but also essential to know how the youth feel and think. Therefore, for further study, I recommend a higher percentage of youth participation in the focus group.

Another recommendation that would boost this project is a session on how to cope with inner church conflict. As previously stated, I assumed the previous pastor was the root of all the issues; however, it soon became evident several internal issues were present as well. Case in point, most of the times there will be division concerning who was at fault and how the pastor was treated. These issues can cause discord within the church. One of the worst things that can happen is for a church to become divided during a crisis. Thus, a session on handling inner church conflict will assist with keeping the church united as they work through situations that may arise in the future.

The final recommendation that would strengthen this project is a session devoted more to ministering to the victims. This project primarily concentrated on healing and rebuilding the church. However, more information or training on how to help the victim would make the project that much more beneficial. When fostering healing to the church, it is critical not to forget the victims involved.

APPENDIX A

PRE AND POST SURVEY

Thank you for participating in this survey. Your participation is anonymous. **PLEASE DO NOT WRITE ANYTHING ON THE SURVEY WHICH MAY BE USED TO IDENTIFY YOU.** The survey has two sections. The first section asks you to rate your knowledge of and feelings toward clergy misconduct. The second section asks for demographic information. Again, thank you for participating in this survey.

SECTION I:

For each item below, **circle the number/statement** that best represents your viewpoint or knowledge.

1 Strongly Disagree   2 Disagree   3 Agree   4 Strongly Agree

1. I have a lot of knowledge about clergy misconduct.

1 Strongly Disagree   2 Disagree   3 Agree   4 Strongly Agree

2. I have a lot of knowledge about how the church should handle clergy misconduct spiritually and legally.

1 Strongly Disagree   2 Disagree   3 Agree   4 Strongly Agree

3. I am still angry or disappointed with the previous pastor:

1 Strongly Disagree   2 Disagree   3 Agree   4 Strongly Agree

4. Clergy who has been found guilty of clergy misconduct can be trusted again.

　　1 Strongly Disagree　2 Disagree　3 Agree　4 Strongly Agree

5. After experiencing clergy misconduct, I do not trust or have confidence in any pastor/clergyperson.

　　1 Strongly Disagree　2 Disagree　3 Agree　4 Strongly Agree

6. I am likely to give clergy a second chance after they have been found guilty of misconduct?

　　1 Strongly Disagree　2 Disagree　3 Agree　4 Strongly Agree

7. Clergy misconduct has lessened my faith in God.

　　1 Strongly Disagree　2 Disagree　3 Agree　4 Strongly Agree

8. I am afraid that clergy misconduct will be repeated in your church.

　　1 Strongly Disagree　2 Disagree　3 Agree　4 Strongly Agree

9. Even years later, I am still ashamed of the clergy misconduct that took place in my church.

    1 Strongly Disagree   2 Disagree   3 Agree   4 Strongly Agree

10. I am pleased with the direction the church is moving under the current pastor.

    1 Strongly Disagree   2 Disagree   3 Agree   4 Strongly Agree

SECTION II:

Directions:
At "A." below, check whether you are male or female.
At "B." below, **MAKE ONE CHECK** at the age group in which you belong.
At "C." below, **WRITE** the number of years of your membership in this church.

A. _____ Male   _____ Female

B. _____ 12-19 _____ 20 – 29 _____ 30 – 39

    _____ 40 – 49 _____ 50 – 59 _____ 60 – 69

    _____ 70 – 79 _____ 80 – 89 _____ 90+

C. _____ years of membership in this church

APPENDIX B

WORKSHOP EVALUATION FORM

Focus Group Workshop Evaluation

Workshop Content	Strongly Agree	Agree	Not Sure	Disagree	Strongly Disagree
1.The information given was relevant to what we have been through as a church.					
2.The information given can be useful in helping the church recover and move forward.					
3.The information given was helpful for me.					
4.The information given was informative and biblically based					

5. The workshop was an effective way to have good dialogue about the information presented					
6. The information presented had an impact on my attitude/opinion					
7. The information challenged me to reconsider some things					
8. This information will help other who experienced clergy misconduct .					

C.) Suggestions: what would have made this presentation better, more useful?_____

_____

_____

_____

_____

_____

_____

_____

_____

_____

Thank you for your contributions

Dr. Vernon D. Shelton, Sr.

BIBLIOGRAPHY

Allen, Leslie C., Timothy Laniak. *New International Biblical Commentary: Ezra, Nehemiah, Esther.* Peabody, MA: Hendrickson Publishers, Inc., 2003.

Ammerman, Nancy Tatom. *Studying Congregations: A New Handbook.* Nashville, TN: Abingdon Press, 1998.

Anderson, Ray Sherman. *The Shape of Practical Theology: Empowering Ministry with Theological Praxis.* Downers Grove, IL: Inter-Varsity Press, 2001.

Andrews, Dale P. *Practical Theology for Black Churches: Bridging Black Theology and African American Religion, 1st edition.* Louisville, KY: Westminster John Knox Press, 2002.

Bainton, Roland Herbert. *Here I Stand: A Life of Martin Luther.* New York: Abingdon-Cokesbury Press, 1950.

Baldwin, Lewis. To Make the Wounded Whole: The Cultural Legacy of Martin Luther King Jr. Minneapolis, MN: Augsburg Fortress, 1992.

Barclay, William. *The Letters to Timothy, Titus, and Philemon. 3rd edition, The New Daily Study Bible.* Louisville: Westminster John Knox Press, 2003.

Bassler, Jouette M. *1 Timothy, 2 Timothy, Titus, Abingdon New Testament Commentaries.* Nashville, TN: Abingdon Press, 1996.

Bausch, William J. *Breaking Trust: A Priest Looks at the Scandal of Sexual Abuse*. Mystic, CT: Twenty-Third Publications, 2002.

Benyei, Candace Reed. *Understanding Clergy Misconduct in Religious Systems: Scapegoating, Family Secrets, and the Abuse of Power*. New York: Haworth Pastoral Press, 1998.

Berry, Jason. *Lead Us Not into Temptation: Catholic Priests and the Sexual Abuse of Children, 1st Illinois paperback edition*. Urbana, IL: University of Illinois Press, 2000.

Birchard, Thaddeus. *"Clergy Sexual Misconduct: frequency and causation."* Sexual and Relationship Therapy, Vol. 15, No.2 (2000):127- 139.

Blenkinsopp, Joseph. *Ezra-Nehemiah: A Commentary, 1st edition, The Old Testament Library*. Philadelphia: Westminster Press, 1988.

Booth, Wayne C., Gregory G. Colomb, and Joseph M. Williams. *The Craft of Research Chicago Guides to Writing, Editing, and Publishing*. Chicago: University of Chicago Press, 1995.

Breneman, Mervin. *Ezra, Nehemiah, Esther The New American Commentary V. 10*. Nashville, TN: Broadman & Holman Publishers, 1993.

Browning, Don S. *Practical Theology,* 1st edition. San Francisco: Harper & Row, 1983.

_____. *A Fundamental Practical Theology: Descriptive and Strategic Proposals*. Minneapolis: Fortress Press, 1991.

Browning, Don S., David Patrick Polk, Ian S. Evison, and University of Chicago. Institute for the Advanced Study of Religion. *The Education of the Practical Theologian:*

Responses to Joseph Hough and John Cobb's Christian Identity and Theological Education Studies in Theological Education. Atlanta, GA: Scholars Press, 1989.

Brueggeman, Walter. *An introduction to the Old Testament: The Canon and Christian to Imagination.* Louisville, KY: Westminster John Knox Press, 2003

Buttrick, George Arthur. *The Interpreter's Bible: The Holy Scriptures in the King James and Revised Standard Versions with General Articles and Introduction, Exegesis, Exposition for Each Book of the Bible.* New York: Abingdon-Cokesbury Press, 1951.

Carnes, Patrick. *Don't Call It Love: Recovery from Sexual Addiction.* New York: Bantam Books, 1991.

Carson, D. A. *New Bible Commentary: 21st Century Edition*, 4th edition. Leicester, England; Downers Grove, IL: Inter-Varsity Press, 1994.

Chaffee, Paul. *Accountable Leadership: A Resource Guide for Sustaining Legal, Financial, and Ethical Integrity in Today's Congregations, 1st edition. The Jossey-Bass Religion-in-Practice Series.* San Francisco, CA: Jossey-Bass Publishers, 1997.

Chrysostom, John, Phillip Schaff. *Nicene and Post-Nicene Father First Series Vol. XIII.* New York: Christian Literature Company, 1889.

Cooper-White, Pamela. *The Cry of Tamar: Violence against Women and the Church's Response.* Minneapolis, MN: Fortress Press, 1995.

Cranton, Patricia. *Professional Development as Transformative Learning: New Perspectives for Teachers of Adults, 1st edition. The Jossey-Bass Higher and Adult Education Series.* San Francisco: Jossey-Bass Publishers, 1996.

Creswell, John W. *Research Design: Qualitative, Quantitative, and Mixed Methods Approaches*. 3rd edition. Thousand Oaks, CA: Sage Publications, 2009.

Cubberley, Ellwood Patterson. *Syllabus of Lectures on the History of Education, with Selected Bibliographies and Suggested Readings*. 2nd edition. London: The Macmillan Company, 1904.

Davies, Gordon F., David W. Cotter, Jerome T. Walsh, and Chris Franke. *Ezra and Nehemiah* Berit Olam. Collegeville, MN: Liturgical Press, 1999.

Davies, Richard E. *Handbook for Doctor of Ministry Projects: An Approach to Structured Observation of Ministry*. Lanham, MD: University Press of America, 1984.

Doyle, Thomas P., A. W. Richard Sipe, and Patrick J. Wall. *Sex, Priests, and Secret Codes: The Catholic Church's 2000-Year Paper Trail of Sexual Abuse*. Los Angeles: Volt Press, 2006.

Dunn, James D. G. *The New Interpreter's Bible: A Commentary In Twelve Volumes, Volume XI*. Nashville, TN: Abingdon Press, 2000.

Dyson, Michael Eric. *I May Not Get There with You: The True Martin Luther King, Jr*. New York: Free Press, 2000.

Everist, Norma Cook. *Church Conflict: From Contention to Collaboration*. Nashville, TN: Abingdon Press, 2004.

Fee, Gordon D. *1 and 2 Timothy, Titus,* 1st edition. A Good News Commentary. San Francisco: Harper & Row, 1984.

Fensham, F. Charles. *The Books of Ezra and Nehemiah* New International Commentary on the Old Testament. Grand Rapids, MI: Erdmans, 1982.

Fiore, Benjamin, and Daniel J. Harrington. *The Pastoral Epistles: First Timothy, Second Timothy, Titus* Sacra Pagina Series. Collegeville, MN: Liturgical Press, 2007.

Flynn, Kathryn A. *The Sexual Abuse of Women by Members of the Clergy.* Jefferson, NC: McFarland & Co., 2003.

Fortune, Marie M. *Sexual Violence: The Unmentionable Sin.* New York: Pilgrim Press, 1983.

_____. *Is Nothing Sacred?: When Sex Invades the Pastoral Relationship,* 1st edition. San Francisco: Harper & Row, 1989.

_____. *Is Nothing Sacred?: The Story of a Pastor, the Women He Sexually Abused, and the Congregation He Nearly Destroyed.* United Church Press ed. Cleveland, OH: United Church Press, 1999.

Fortune, Marie M., and W. Merle Longwood. *Sexual Abuse in the Catholic Church: Trusting the Clergy?* Binghamton, NY: Haworth Pastoral Press, 2003.

Fortune, Marie M., and Joretta L. Marshall. *Forgiveness and Abuse: Jewish and Christian Reflections.* New York: Haworth Pastoral Press, 2002.

Frawley-O'Dea, Mary Gail. *Perversion of Power: Sexual Abuse in the Catholic Church.* 1st edition. Nashville, TN: Vanderbilt University Press, 2007.

Frawley-O'Dea, Mary Gail, and Virginia Goldner. *Predatory Priests, Silenced Victims: The Sexual Abuse Crisis and the Catholic Church.* Mahwah, NJ: Analytic Press, 2007.

Friberg, Nils, Nancy Myer Hopkins, Mark R. Laaser, and Interfaith Sexual Trauma Institute (Collegeville, MN). *Restoring the Soul of a Church: Healing Congregations Wounded by*

Clergy Sexual Misconduct. Collegeville, MN: Liturgical Press, 1995.

Friberg, Nils, and Mark R. Laaser. *Before the Fall: Preventing Pastoral Sexual Abuse.* Collegeville, MN: Liturgical Press, 1998.

Gaede, Beth Ann, and Candace Reed Benyei. *When a Congregation Is Betrayed: Responding to Clergy Misconduct.* Herndon, VA: Alban Institute, 2006.

Gloer, W. Hulitt. 1&2 Timothy-Titus. Macon, GA: Smyth & Helwys Publishing, Inc., 2010.

Grab, Wilhelm. *Secularization Theories, Religious Identity and Practical Theology.* Berlin: Lit Verlag GMBH & CO., 2009

Grabbe, Lester L. *Ezra-Nehemiah: Old Testament Readings.* New York: Routledge, 1998.

Greenwood, Davydd J., and Morten Levin. *Introduction to Action Research: Social Research for Social Change,* 2nd edition. Thousand Oaks, CA: Sage Publications, 2007.

Grenz, Stanley J., and Roy D. Bell. *Betrayal of Trust: Confronting and Preventing Sexual Misconduct.* Grand Rapids, MI: Baker Publishing Group, 2001.

Guinness, Os, Virginia Mooney, and Karen Lee-Thorp. *Steering through Chaos!: Vice and Virtue in an Age of Moral Confusion.* The Trinity Forum Study Series. Colorado Springs, CO: Nav-Press, 2000.

Gula, Richard M. *Ethics in Pastoral Ministry.* New York: Paulist Press, 1996.

_____. *The Call to Holiness: Embracing a Fully Christian Life*. New York: Paulist Press, 2003.

Guthrie, Donald. *The Pastoral Epistles: An Introduction and Commentary Tyndale New Testament Commentaries*. Nottingham, England Downers Grove, IL: Inter-Varsity Press; Intervarsity Press, 2009.

Hanson, Anthony Tyrrell. *The New Century Bible Commentary: The Pastoral Epistles*. Grand Rapids, MI: Wm. B. Eerdmans Publishing Company, 1982.

Harris, James H. *Pastoral Theology: A Black-Church Perspective*. Minneapolis, MN: Fortress Press, 1991.

Hayes, Carlton J. H. *A Political and Cultural History of Modern Europe*. New York: Published for the United States Armed Forces Institute by Macmillan, 1944.

Hedges-Goettl, Len, and Daniel G. Bagby. *Sexual Abuse: Pastoral Responses*. Nashville, TN: Abingdon Press, 2004.

Heitink, Gerben. *Practical Theology: History, Theory, Action Domains: Manual for Practical Theology* Studies in Practical Theology. Grand Rapids, MI: W.B. Eerdmans Pub. Co., 1999.

Holmgren, Fredrick Carlson. *Israel Alive Again: A Commentary on the Books of Ezra and Nehemiah* International Theological Commentary. Grand Rapids Edinburgh: W.B. Eerdmans Pub. Co., Handsel Press, 1987.

Hopkins, Dwight N., and Anthony B. Pinn. *Loving the Body: Black Religious Studies and the Erotic,* 1st edition. Black Religion, Womanist Thought, Social Justice. New York: Palgrave Macmillan, 2004.

Hopkins, Nancy Myer, and Interfaith Sexual Trauma Institute (Collegeville Minn.). *The Congregational Response to*

Clergy Betrayals of Trust. Collegeville, MN: Liturgical Press, 1998.

Horst, Elisabeth A. *Questions and Answers About Clergy Sexual Misconduct*. Collegeville, MN: Liturgical Press, 2000.

Horst, Elisabeth A., and Interfaith Sexual Trauma Institute (Collegeville, MN). *Recovering the Lost Self: Shame-Healing for Victims of Clergy Sexual Abuse*. Collegeville, MN: Liturgical Press, 1998.

Houlden, J. L. *The Pastoral Epistles: I and Ii Timothy, Titus* TPI New Testament Commentaries. London Philadelphia: SCM Press; Trinity Press International, 1989.

Hultgren, Arland J. *Augsburg Commentary on the New Testament:I-II Timothy, Titus*. Minneapolis, MN: Augsburg Publishing House, 1984.

International Bible Society. *Vox Dei: Holy Bible, New International Version*. Colorado Springs, CO: International Bible Society, 1993.

Karris, Robert J. *The Pastoral Epistles*. Wilmington, DE: Michael Glazier, 1979.

Keenan, James F., and Joseph J. Kotva. *Practice What You Preach: Virtues, Ethics, and Power in the Lives of Pastoral Ministers and Their Congregations*. Franklin, WI: Sheed & Ward, 1999.

Kelly, J. N. D. *A Commentary on the Pastoral Epistles: I Timothy, II Timothy, Titus* Black's New Testament Commentaries. London: A. & C. Black, 1963.

King, J. L. *On The Down Low: A Journey Into The Lives Of Straight Black Men Who Sleep With Men*. Harlem, NY: Harlem Moon, 2005.

Klein, Ralph W. *The New Interpreter's Bible: A Commentary In Twelve Volumes, Volume III.* Nashville, TN: Abingdon Press, 1999.

Knight, George W. *Commentary on the Pastoral Epistles.* Grand Rapids, MI: Wm. B. Eerdmans Publishing Company, 1992.

Larson, Knute, Kathy Dahlen, and Max E. Anders. *Ezra, Nehemiah, Esther* Holman Old Testament Commentary V. 9. Nashville, TN: Broadman & Holman, 2005.

Lea, Thomas D., and Hayne P. Griffin. *1, 2 Timothy, Titus* The New American Commentary V. 34. Nashville, TN: Broadman Press, 1992.

Lebacqz, Karen. *Professional Ethics: Power and Paradox.* Nashville, TN: Abingdon Press, 1985.

Lebacqz, Karen, and Ronald G. Barton. *Sex in the Parish.* 1st edition. Louisville, KY: Westminster/J. Knox Press, 1991.

Levering, Matthew. *Ezra & Nehemiah* Brazos Theological Commentary on the Bible. Grand Rapids, MI: Brazos Press, 2007.

Lewis, G. Douglass. *Resolving Church Conflicts: A Case Study Approach for Local Congregations.* 1st edition. San Francisco: Harper and Row, 1981.

Lief, Harold. "*Boundary Crossings: Sexual Misconduct of Clergy.*" Journal of Sex Education And Therapy, Vol.26, No.4 (2001): 310-314.

Liefeld, Walter L. *1 and 2 Timothy/Titus: The Niv Application Commentary from Biblical Text--to Contemporary Life* The Niv Application Commentary Series. Grand Rapids, MI: Zondervan, 1999.

Lincoln, C. Eric, and Lawrence H. Mamiya. *The Black Church in the African-American Experience*. Durham, NC: Duke University Press, 1990.

Lohse, Bernhard. *Martin Luther: An Introduction to His Life and Work*. Philadelphia: Fortress Press, 1986.

Lyon, K. Brynolf, and Don S. Browning. *Toward a Practical Theology of Aging* Theology and Pastoral Care. Philadelphia: Fortress Press, 1985.

Mann, Thomas. *The Oxford Guide to Library Research*, 3rd edition. New York: Oxford University Press, 2005.

McConville, J. G. *Ezra, Nehemiah, and Esther* Daily Study Bible-- Old Testament. Philadelphia: Westminster Press, 1985.

McGrath, Alister E. *Christian Theology: An Introduction,* 3rd edition. Oxford; Malden, MA: Blackwell Publishers, 2001.

McKim, Donald K. *Theological Turning Points: Major Issues in Christian Thought*. Atlanta, GA: John Knox Press, 1988.

_____. *Westminster Dictionary of Theological Terms*. 1st edition. Louisville, KY: Westminster John Knox Press, 1996.

_____. *The Westminster Handbook to Reformed Theology*. 1st edition. The Westminster Handbooks to Christian Theology. Louisville, KY: Westminster John Knox Press, 2001.

McNiff, Jean, Pamela Lomax, and Jack Whitehead. *You and Your Action Research Project*. 2nd edition. London; New York: Routledge Falmer, 2003.

Miles, Matthew B., and A. M. Huberman. *Qualitative Data Analysis: An Expanded Sourcebook.* 2nd edition. Thousand Oaks: Sage Publications, 1994.

Miles, Rebekah. *The Pastor as Moral Guide* Creative Pastoral Care and Counseling. Minneapolis, MN: Fortress Press, 1999.

Mitchell, Timothy. *Betrayal of the Innocents: Desire, Power, and the Catholic Church in Spain.* Philadelphia: University of Pennsylvania Press, 1998.

Mosgofian, Peter T., and George W. Ohlschlager. *Sexual Misconduct in Counseling and Ministry* Contemporary Christian Counseling 10. Dallas, TX: Word, 1995.

Müller-Fahrenholz, Geiko. *The Art of Forgiveness: Theological Reflections on Healing and Reconciliation.* Geneva: WCC Publications, 1997.

Myers, Jacob Martin. *Ezra. Nehemiah.* 1st edition. The Anchor Bible, Garden City, NY: Doubleday, 1965.

Noss, Philip A., and Kenneth J. Thomas. *A Handbook on Ezra and Nehemiah,* Ubs Handbook Series. New York: United Bible Societies, 2005.

Nouwen, Henri J. M. *The Wounded Healer: Ministry in Contemporary Society,* 1st edition. Garden City, NY: Doubleday, 1972.

Oden, Thomas C. *First and Second Timothy and Titus,* Interpretation, a Bible Commentary for Teaching and Preaching. Louisville, KY: J. Knox Press, 1989.

Ormerod, Neil, and Thea Ormerod. *When Ministers Sin: Sexual Abuse in the Churches.* Alexandria, NSW, Australia Cincinnati, OH: Millennium Books; Distributed in the U.S. by Seven Hills Book Distributors, 1995.

Osborne, Larry W. *Sticky Teams: Keeping Your Leadership Team and Staff on the Same Page*. Grand Rapids, MI: Zondervan, 2010.

Osmer, Richard Robert. *Practical Theology: An Introduction*. Grand Rapids, MI: William B. Eerdmans Pub. Co., 2008.

Panichas, George. *"Scandals in the Church."* Modern Age: A Quarterly Review (Fall 2002): 299-303.

Park, Andrew Sung. *From Hurt to Healing: A Theology of the Wounded*. Nashville, TN: Abingdon Press, 2004.

Peters, Dave. *Surviving Church Conflict*. Scottdale, PA: Herald Press, 1997.

Pohly, Kenneth H. *Transforming the Rough Places: The Ministry of Supervision*. Franklin, TN: Providence House, 2001.

Poirier, Alfred. *The Peacemaking Pastor: A Biblical Guide to Resolving Church Conflict*. Grand Rapids, MI: Baker Books, 2006.

Poling, James N. *Rethinking Faith: A Constructive Practical Theology*. Minneapolis: Fortress Press, 2011.

Poling, James N., and Donald E. Miller. *Foundations for a Practical Theology of Ministry*. Nashville, TN: Abingdon Press, 1985.

Proctor, Samuel D. *The Certain Sound of the Trumpet: Crafting Sermons of Authority*. Valley Forge, PA: Judson Press, 1994.

_____*The Substance of Things Hoped For:A Memoir* of *African-American Faith*. Valley Forge, PA: Judson Press, 1999.

Quinn, Jerome D. T*he Anchor Bible: The Letter To Titus.* New York, NY: Doubleday, 1990.

Ragsdale, Katherine Hancock. *Boundary Wars: Intimacy and Distance in Healing Relationships.* Cleveland, OH: Pilgrim Press, 1996.

Rediger, G. Lloyd. *Beyond the Scandals: A Guide to Healthy Sexuality for Clergy Prisms.* Minneapolis: Fortress Press, 2003.

Richards, Nancy, and Marie M. Fortune. *Heal and Forgive: Forgiveness in the Face of Abuse.* Nevada City, CA: Blue Dolphin Publishing, Inc., 2005.

Richardson, Ronald W. *Creating a Healthier Church: Family Systems Theory, Leadership, and Congregational Life* Creative Pastoral Care and Counseling Series. Minneapolis: Fortress Press, 1996.

_____. *Becoming a Healthier Pastor: Family Systems Theory and the Pastor's Own Family* Creative Pastoral Care and Counseling Series. Minneapolis: Fortress Press, 2005.

Robinson, James Harvey. *Medieval and Modern Times; an Introduction to the History of Western Europe Form the Dissolution of the Roman Empire to the Present Time. Rev. to include the great war, 1914-1918. edition.* Boston, New York, etc.: Ginn and company, 1919.

Robinson, Linda Hansen. *"The Abuse of Power: A View of Sexual Misconduct in a Systemic Approach to Pastoral Care."* Pastoral Psychology, Vol. 52, No. 5 (May 2004): 395-404.

Saarinen, Risto. *The Pastoral Epistles with Philemon & Jude* Brazos Theological Commentary on the Bible. Grand Rapids, MI: Brazos Press, 2008.

Sande, Ken. *The Peacemaker: A Biblical Guide to Resolving Personal Conflict.* 3rd edition. Grand Rapids, MI: Baker Books, 2004.

Schenck, Ferdinand Schureman. *Modern Practical Theology; a Manual of Homiletics, Liturgics, Poimenics, Archagics, Pedagogy, Sociology, and the English Bible.* New York, London: Funk & Wagnalls company, 1903.

Scott, E.F. *The Moffatt New Testament Commentary: The Pastoral Epistles.* London: Hodder And Stoughton, 1947.

Serstock, Jan Johansen. *When I Was First Alone: A Journey from Hurt to Healing.* San Antonio, TX: LangMarc Pub., 1993.

Shelley, Marshall. *Leading Your Church through Conflict and Reconciliation: 30 Strategies to Transform Your Ministry* Library of Leadership Development 1. Minneapolis, MN: Bethany House Publishers, 1997.

Shupe, Anson D. *In the Name of All That's Holy: A Theory* of *Clergy Malfeasance.* Westport, CT: Praeger, 1995.

————. *Wolves within the Fold: Religious Leadership and Abuses of Power.* New Brunswick, NJ: Rutgers University Press, 1998.

————. *Spoils of the Kingdom: Clergy Misconduct and Religious Community.*
Urbana, IL: University of Illinois Press, 2007.

Shupe, Anson D., William A. Stacey, and Susan E. Darnell. *Bad Pastors: Clergy Misconduct in Modern America.* New York: New York University Press, 2000.

Smith, Donald P. *Congregations Alive.* 1st edition. Philadelphia: Westminster Press, 1981.

Steinke, Peter L. *Congregational Leadership in Anxious Times: Being Calm and Courageous No Matter What*. Herndon, VA: Alban Institute, 2006.

_____. *Healthy Congregations: A Systems Approach,* 2nd edition. Herndon, VA: Alban Institute, 2006.

_____. *How Your Church Family Works: Understanding Congregations as Emotional Systems*. Herndon, VA: Alban Institute, 2006.

Stetzer, Ed, and Mike Dodson. *Comeback Churches: How 300 Churches Turned around and Yours Can Too*. Nashville, TN: B & H Pub. Group, 2007.

Swindoll, Charles R. *Hand Me Another Brick*. Nashville, TN: Nelson, 1990.

_____. *Hand Me Another Brick: Timeless Lessons on Leadership: How Effective Leaders Motivate Themselves and Others*. Nashville, TN: W Pub. Group, 2006.

Thomas. *Commentaries on St. Paul's Epistles to Timothy, Titus, and Philemon*. South Bend, IN: St. Augustine's Press, 2007.

Thomas, Owen C., and Ellen K. Wondra. *Introduction to Theology,* 3rd edition. Harrisburg, PA: Morehouse, 2002.

Throntveit, Mark A. *Ezra-Nehemiah: Interpretation, a Bible Commentary for Teaching and Preaching*. Louisville, KY: John Knox Press, 1992.

Tiffany, Frederick C., and Sharon H. Ringe. *Biblical Interpretation: A Roadmap*. Nashville, TN: Abingdon Press, 1996.

Tracy, Steven R. *Mending the Soul: Understanding and Healing Abuse,* 1st edition. Grand Rapids, MI: Zondervan, 2005.

Trull, Joe E., and James E. Carter. *Ministerial Ethics: Moral Formation for Church Leaders,* 2nd edition. Grand Rapids, MI: Baker Academic, 2004.

Turabian, Kate L. *A Manual for Writers of Research Papers, Theses, and Dissertations: Chicago Style for Students and Researchers,* 7th edition. Chicago Guides to Writing, Editing, and Publishing. Chicago: University of Chicago Press, 2007.

Van Wijk-Bos, Johanna W. H. *Ezra, Nehemiah, and Esther,* 1st edition. Westminster Bible Companion. Louisville, KY: Westminster John Knox Press, 1998.

Viau, Marcel. *Practical Theology: A New Approach* Empirical Studies in Theology. Leiden; Boston, MA: Brill, 1999.

Volf, Miroslav, and Dorothy C. Bass. *Practicing Theology: Beliefs and Practices in Christian Life.* Grand Rapids, MI: W.B. Eerdmans, 2002.

Vyhmeister, Nancy J. *Quality Research Papers for Students of Religion and Theology.* 2nd edition. Grand Rapids, MI: Zondervan, 2008.

Walker, Williston. *A History of the Christian Church,* 4th edition. Edinburgh: T. & T. Clark, 1986.

Walvoord, John F., Roy B. Zuck, and Dallas Theological Seminary. *The Bible Knowledge Commentary: An Exposition of the Scriptures.* 2 vols. Wheaton, IL: Victor Books, 1983.

Wiersbe, W. W. *Be Determined.* Wheaton, IL: Victor Books, 1996.

Wiggins, Daphne C. *Righteous Content: Black Women's Perspectives of Church and Faith.* New York: New York University Press, 2005.

Wilson, Earl D. *Restoring the Fallen: A Team Approach to Caring, Confronting & Reconciling.* Downers Grove, IL: InterVarsity Press, 1997.

Wilson, Scott. *Steering through Chaos: Mapping a Clear Direction for Your Church in the Midst of Transition and Change.* Grand Rapids, MI: Zondervan, 2009.

Winebrenner, Jan, and Debra Frazier. *When a Leader Falls: What Happens to Everyone Else?* Minneapolis, MN: Bethany House, 1993.

Wolcott, Harry F. *Writing up Qualitative Research* Qualitative Research Methods V. 20. Newbury Park, CA: Sage Publications, 1990.

Young, Frances M. *The Theology of the Pastoral Letters.* Cambridge: Cambridge University Press Cambridge, 1994.

ABOUT THE AUTHOR

Dr. Vernon D. Shelton, Sr. was born on April 24, 1975 in Baltimore, MD and raised in the Park Heights Community. He attended Coppin State University where he earned a Bachelor of Science in Criminal Justice. An avid athlete, Shelton played for Coppin's baseball team under former Orioles center fielder Paul Blair; and eventually, he went on to play semi-pro baseball in the state of Maryland. In 2006, Dr. Shelton earned a Master's of Divinity degree at The Samuel Dewitt Proctor School of Theology at Virginia Union University Seminary. In June of 2012, Dr. Shelton earned Doctorate of Ministry degree from the United Theological Seminary, in Dayton Ohio.

Dr. Shelton received and accepted the call to the preaching ministry at the age of 26, and preached his initial sermon on March 1, 2002 at

Jerusalem Baptist Church. From 2006 to 2010, Dr. Shelton served as the Senior Pastor of The New Hope Christian Baptist Church in Baltimore, Maryland. On September 19, 2010 Dr. Shelton was installed as the tenth pastor of the Holy Trinity Baptist Church in Amityville, NY. During the first year of Dr. Shelton's arrival, Holy Trinity experienced significant growth, spiritually and numerically with over 150 disciples joining the church; 70 as candidates for baptism. Dr. Shelton has revived, restored hope, financial stability, and a spirit of excellence in the Holy Trinity Baptist Church since his arrival.

He is a member of the Kingdom Association of Covenant Pastors (KACP) under Bishop Walter S. Thomas, Sr. He is also an active member of the Eastern Baptist Association, and many other community organizations in the Amityville area. Dr. Shelton is a firm believer that every aspect of life and ministry should be done in excellence. His favorite motto is *"Excellence is not the standard, but the minimum."* He is a devoted husband to his wife, LaPrena, and the proud father of Terrance, Monique, Myriah *(stepdaughter)*, Ayona, and Vernon, Jr.

Dr. Shelton's favorite scripture is: *"The Spirit of the Lord is on me, because He has anointed me to preach good news to the poor. He has sent me to proclaim freedom for the prisoners and recovery of sight for the blind, to release the oppressed, to proclaim the year of the Lord's favor."* **Luke 4:18-19**